The Foundation of Success

Business Based on Trust and Understanding

By John J. Kim

With a Foreword by Les Schlais

© 2012 Syncis, Inc.

All rights reserved. Except as permitted under U.S. copyright law, no part of this book may be used or reproduced in any manner without written permission.

The views expressed herein are those of the author and do not necessarily reflect the views or policies of Syncis, Inc., and its affiliates or any other organization. Nothing herein is intended to form a contractual agreement or to modify or to supplement any existing contractual agreement. This publication is sold with the understanding that the publisher and author are not engaged in rendering legal, accounting, or other professional services.

Some names and identifying details have been changed to protect the privacy of individuals. Although the author and publisher have made every effort to ensure the accuracy and completeness of the information contained in this book, we assume no responsibility for errors, inaccuracies, omissions, or inconsistencies herein.

Editing by Thomas B. Kim and Susan Y. Kim with Lawrence Ineno

Cover design and illustrations by Eun Hye "Grace" Lee

The Foundation of Success:
Business Based on Trust and Understanding

Syncis, Inc.
Gardena, CA USA
www.syncis.com

ISBN: 9780615720487
LCCN: 2012953455

Printed and bound in the United States of America

Dedication and Acknowledgments

This book is a result of years of knowledge and inspiration gained from talking to and learning from people from all walks of life. I would like to thank everyone who taught me to be a stronger leader, teacher, mentor, and student. I would especially like to thank my business partner, Les Schlais, who inspires and pushes me to be better. I also would like to thank everyone who helped me write this book. Without your support, this book could not have happened.

To everyone reading this book: I hope what you discover in this book will inspire you to start your own business adventure and become more successful than even I can dream.

—John J. Kim

Table of Contents

Foreword	A Rhino Stumbling Forward, by Les Schlais	1
Part 1	**The Foundation of Success**	11
Chapter 1	Trust and Understanding	13
Chapter 2	The Importance of a Mindset and System	39
Chapter 3	The Green Button Checklist	51
Part 2	**Basic Training**	61
Chapter 4	An Introduction to Basic Training	63
Chapter 5	The Home Visit	69
Chapter 6	The Personal Financial Checkup (PFC)	73
Chapter 7	The Associate Checklist	83
Chapter 8	The Leverage Exchange	87
Chapter 9	Warm Market Prospecting	97
Chapter 10	Prospect List and Hot Buttons	105
Chapter 11	Appointments	121
Chapter 12	Business Presentation Meeting (BPM)	137
Chapter 13	Events	149
Chapter 14	Referrals	153
Chapter 15	Accountability	161
Chapter 16	Team Builder's Club	167
Chapter 17	When the Student Becomes a Teacher	173
Part 3	**Leadership Training**	177
Chapter 18	Leaders Are Created, Not Born	179
Chapter 19	Leadership Strategy	189
Chapter 20	The 7 Point List	203
Chapter 21	Leadership Layers	219
Chapter 22	The Natural Teamwork Approach	227
Chapter 23	Trust the System	235

Foreword

A Rhino Stumbling Forward

Shortly after I met John Kim, I realized that his vision for building a strong organization was completely different from anything I'd seen in my many years in the financial services industry. Considering that I'd spent my entire career studying countless business strategies, worked with national leaders in sales and management, and had been a top producer in a very competitive profession, I was pretty sure I'd never hear anything new that would capture my complete attention.

After constantly being pitched the "latest and greatest" sales strategies, I'd grown used to thinking that the so-called latest and greatest was never anything new at all. So when I heard about this crazy guy out in Los Angeles named John Kim, I was skeptical.

At the same time, despite my doubts, I'd always had an open mind, and I was constantly in search of new ways to grow my business—which probably explains why I felt so confident that I'd heard about every business-building strategy on Earth!

While many people would be happy switching roles with me—I had done well in my career and had mentored countless individuals—I knew that there was more for me to accomplish and new journeys for me to take. So I decided to learn more about John Kim, and it turned out to be one of the best career moves I've ever made.

My Definition of Success

From the start of my professional life, I knew that I wanted to be successful, and I had also defined what that meant to me. I saw people working for their employers for decades and getting nowhere, which wasn't my definition of success. I wanted a business that I didn't need to babysit every hour of every day. In other words, success meant taking on the role of an owner rather than an employee. But I quickly learned how difficult playing that role would be—no wonder so many people say, "I want to be my own boss," yet so few people actually accomplish this.

Even many highly paid professionals, such as doctors, *think* they run a true business, but in a way they don't. After all, what would happen if a physician with a solo practice didn't show up to work? The doctor's patients wouldn't receive services, and his or her income would suffer. That wasn't the type of business I was looking for. From my perspective, professionals like these were just another example of employees tied to a business. Only in this case, they had the luxury of having their names on the doors of their offices.

So when I joined the financial services industry, I thought I had found the perfect fit. This career path provided the opportunity to earn a solid income by running a large sales team. In addition, it had the potential to be self-sustaining. In other words, business would continue even if I wasn't watching it every second of every day.

So for about twenty years, I chased my dream. Unfortunately, without knowing it, I did it the wrong way. I was like a rhino stumbling forward through the industry without putting a lot of thought into how my business was running. From the start, I followed a flawed team-building approach that other major organizations had taught their sales staff: Recruit as many people as possible and worry about the details later. I became very good at recruiting people to join my sales team. In fact, at one point I was managing hundreds of representatives at over 50 locations across the country. I was generously rewarded for my hard work, and I was rising to the top of my industry. *Unfortunately, I was also exhausted and didn't know how much longer I could maintain the heavy workload.*

My Turning Point

When I met John Kim and learned about his background, I believed that he embodied the American Dream. John was an immigrant who was raised in South Korea. He arrived in the U.S. speaking little English and with very little money. What he did have was an appetite for knowledge and a strong work ethic.

Within a few minutes of speaking to John and listening to his ideas about business, I realized that his approach to team building and leadership was unlike anything I had ever heard before. In addition, when he and I met, what stood out in my mind was his ability to connect with me right away. He had an amazing ability to ask questions that made me challenge my beliefs.

He first asked about my career path, and I shared what I had accomplished: I was proud that I had built and led a sales team that had hundreds of representatives, and I told him about the great income I was making. But for some reason, none of this impressed him.

"Sounds great. But do you know how to really build?" John asked me. I had a team with hundreds of representatives, so the answer seemed obvious. My response, however, didn't satisfy him.

"I don't think you understand what I'm saying," he said. "You're good at what you do, and you've made a lot of money. But you still don't know how to build teams that last," he said.

"Of course I know how to build lasting teams," I said. "I've managed a ton of people throughout my career. In fact, people constantly want to go into business with me."

"You still don't understand what I mean," he said.

John then explained that he'd spent years following the same business approach that I'd stuck to. Thus he knew every aspect of the team-building method that I'd grown to rely on—one that had been the foundation of my success.

"Let me put it to you this way—the system we've been taught by the industry has serious problems. And I guarantee if you're honest, you'll agree with what I'm saying." He then pointed out the following weaknesses of the recruiting approach that we'd both learned from other companies in the industry.

High Turnover

From a numbers perspective, my team looked BIG. But what the numbers *didn't show* was that almost all of my team eventually left after a few months. And I was tired of replacing those who had quit.

Low Loyalty

If members of my team believed that there were even slightly better opportunities waiting for them, they'd take advantage of them and leave me—which meant that they didn't feel any commitment to the organization or to me.

No Independence

The team-building system that I'd learned and followed didn't lead to independence for my team members. So my team always depended on me to solve its problems and take charge of things when they went wrong—*and things seemed to go wrong all the time!* The classroom training and licenses didn't prepare them to deal with real-world situations or to think of creative solutions.

Short-Term Success

Although I earned a good income, I still had to be working 100 percent of the time in order for my business to operate smoothly. I didn't know how much longer I could last because fixing problems within my team limited my ability to grow, and it also left me worn out.

John clearly had gone through exactly what I had. And by the expression on my face, I'm sure John knew that his words connected with me. "Isn't it time to try an approach that doesn't have so many problems?" he asked.

John then shared his strategy—a business model that had relationships at its foundation. He explained that when relationships were the core of my team, everyone would be loyal to both each other and the organization. In other words, John's system was based on a version of teamwork that was completely new to me. His approach could be summarized with these words: **Trust and Understanding**.

After talking with him about business, I felt as if I had had a sickness for years, and a doctor finally was able to tell me what was wrong. Not only that, but he also provided a cure. For the first time, someone had pointed out what was missing in my business: *relationships based on Trust and Understanding.*

Soon after our initial meeting, John invited me to see how his system looked in his everyday life. I visited his office to watch how he worked. Watching John interact with strangers and seeing how he quickly earned their trust convinced me that he had developed a powerful way to connect with others. I could tell that from an outside point of view, the system seemed simple. But I also knew better. Although the steps were easy to explain, mastering them would require hard work and focus. I couldn't wait to use his approach to build a better team.

Why Should You Read This Book?

The method that John Kim will describe in the following pages is changing the way that motivated people, like you, connect with their team members and clients. After reading this book, you'll have the proven tools that have created strong teams and long-term results.

Most of us don't know how to build lasting relationships with our clients and business associates. This makes sense because we were never shown how. This book teaches you something that most other businesses only pay lip service to: Successful relationships are based on building **Trust and Understanding**—from the start. Throughout this book, you'll learn what a training system based on Trust and Understanding is, why it's important, and how to make it the foundation of a successful business.

How to Get the Most Out of This Book

When I first partnered with John, I was already a believer in his system, and I was eager to spread it nationwide. We worked together, pooled our strengths, and developed a program that would be easy for others to learn.

Unfortunately, what we saw over and over was that new team members constantly found themselves falling into bad habits that were based on their past experiences. Sometimes they did this on purpose because they thought their way was better and made more sense. Other times, it was just out of sticking to their old routines for so long. In either case, they made mistakes that were completely avoidable had they fully embraced our approach.

That's why I urge you to not "reinvent the wheel." In other words, avoid ignoring what's in this book because you're convinced that your way is better. And I say this because I was guilty of being a "wheel reinventor." What you're reading is based on principles that have resulted in incredible success for people just like you and me. Following the approach that John describes also prevents the common mistakes that many people have made over the years. The bottom line is that there's no point in slowing yourself down with mistakes that you can easily prevent. So save yourself the heartache, and even when you're doubtful about the system, just follow it anyway. Take a "leap of faith" and "stumble forward"—in other words, ignore doubts you have and fully trust that success is within your reach. I assure you that everything you learn will make sense to you later, and you'll be glad that you listened to my recommendation.

Finally, my advice to you is to open your mind and heart to the approach that's described in these pages. I say this because there will be times when you may be confused or experience doubt about the business-building principles presented in this book. This is a natural part of learning a completely new way of working. But resist the temptation to do things differently or to skip steps. Believe in the system, even when it doesn't seem logical, and I'm 100 percent convinced that everything will work out eventually. I say this with such certainty because I've seen the system change the lives of people from diverse backgrounds. In fact, there will come a point at which you'll wonder how you ever worked any other way.

The entire system that John describes in this book is built on the wisdom, insights, and mistakes of those who have come before you. In the end, this book will change the way you think, the way you build relationships, and the way you do business. So get ready to learn what can help you achieve success beyond what you thought was possible for you and those you care about.

—Les Schlais

Part 1
The Foundation of Success

Chapter 1

Trust and Understanding: Uncovering the Secrets of Success

I was at a convention a few years ago when I realized that I needed to completely change the foundation of my business.

During one of the convention's meetings, a woman nervously walked to the stage and accepted an award as the top salesperson in the company that I was working with at the time. The announcer asked Jane to share a few words. She described how, just a few years ago, she would have never imagined receiving the top award.

"Right out of high school I got married, and shortly after I became a mom. After that, I quit working to raise my kids. When they were older, I wanted to start a new career to help with the bills. I hadn't worked for years, but a friend introduced me to this business, and I decided to give it a try. That was about a year ago," she said.

"Give it a try?" I thought to myself. She sounded so casual about her start, which frustrated me. I was someone who had spent countless hours thinking and debating before deciding to join the financial industry. I spent years developing my skills, earning multiple licenses, and learning everything possible about the products—basically, I did everything that I was supposed to. I didn't have to rely on anyone for help because I felt I had the knowledge to do everything myself.

Meanwhile, Jane seemed to have found this career and industry by accident. Where was her dedication? Where was her struggle to rise to the top? Based on her speech, it didn't sound as though she had worked as hard as I had. The truth is, her speech annoyed me a little bit. At the same time, I had to admit that Jane was far more successful than I was at the time.

I was very proud to have a couple of team members with me at that convention. Jane, on the other hand, probably had over 200 people cheering for her. I was pleased that many people respected my knowledge. But Jane was the one winning the major company award. Next, I thought that I was earning a good income. Jane, however, was probably making ten times more money than me based on the size of her team. The bottom line was that my ego told me that I was far more successful and far more talented than I really was. Jane's success had humbled me, and I needed to learn how she won that award.

Jane's Secret

Conventions like these provide many opportunities for networking. But I'm a shy guy—even today—so at the time, I wasn't sure I should talk to her. After thinking about it, I decided I really needed to know her secret, so I introduced myself to Jane and congratulated her for her award. As a salesperson, I was well trained in "reading people." In other words, I learned to make decisions about others based on what they said as well as by the expressions on their faces. It was obvious to me that Jane was kind, humble, and honest. Her sincerity and warmth made me relax and allowed me to ask her what I'd been wondering all along.

"Jane, if you don't mind the question...how did you win that award?" I asked.

"First off, I didn't do it on my own. In fact, I owe it all to my team. When I started my career, I knew early on that there was no way that I could do this by myself. Even if I learned everything about products and spent hours in corporate training, I was only one person with limited time and energy," she said.

She went on to explain that one of her biggest strengths was her ability to know what she was good at, which also meant that she knew her weaknesses. "And I had no problem working with people who were clearly better than I was at certain things."

Over time, Jane built and led a team in which everyone trusted and depended on one another. "Each person on my team had something important to provide. And we all knew it. We all counted on each other to do what each of us did best. As a result, we achieved far more together than we could have by ourselves. I know some people here might know more than me or have better skills. But combined, my team is better than anyone else here. My team and the trust and understanding we have are *the foundation of my success,*" she said.

My Turning Point

By seeing both her strengths and weaknesses, Jane was able to focus on how to grow her business. She didn't waste her time trying to do everything on her own. Instead, she worked hard to make her strengths even stronger and found others to fill in areas where she needed help. As a result of meeting Jane, I asked myself, "What are my talents and skills? And how can I use these to build the best business?"

I realized that the answer would only come if I took an honest look at my strengths *and* weaknesses. To do that, I started looking at my past.

I was born and raised in South Korea, a country with many traditions that are familiar to anyone who grew up in the U.S. For example, both nations have democratic governments, skilled workforces, and strong economies. At the same time, there are many differences between the two countries.

When I was growing up, the South Korean government was always in a "state of war" with North Korea. Therefore, from an early age, I was taught the importance of discipline and staying connected with my fellow citizens. My culture rewarded those who stayed focused and followed the rules, and it looked down upon those who tried to set their own paths and break from very old traditions.

In addition, my culture taught me to work hard and to not ask others for help. But for all its benefits, not seeking help can also be a weakness. I realized that it kept me from doing what made Jane so successful—she counted on others to strengthen areas where she was weak. In addition, my background caused me to ignore ideas that were different from what I was used to.

As the saying goes, "The truth will set you free." In other words, once I identified my strengths and weaknesses, I was free to change the way I did business.

By being totally honest with myself, I became open-minded and saw new possibilities.

I thought to myself, "What if I combined the strengths of my two cultures: South Korea and the United States?" I imagined what would happen if I blended the limitless opportunities and creativity of U.S. culture with the discipline and focus of South Korea. Over the next few years, I created a unique business system for building a successful team that is the foundation of my success today. What you're reading now is the system that I developed, and it's based on two simple beliefs: Building a successful team requires **Trust and Understanding**, and a successful team can accomplish more than any single individual.

Sadly, many companies throughout the U.S. operate in a different way. Customers don't trust businesses, employees don't trust their bosses, and bosses often don't understand the needs of their staff and clients. That is why, in most businesses, people are focused on helping only themselves and unintentionally become enemies with everyone else. In contrast, I strongly believe that if leaders and everyone else within an organization focused on building **Trust and Understanding** with their colleagues and customers, companies across the U.S. would be more caring, more responsible, and more successful.

Trust and Understanding Start from Within

In order to build Trust and Understanding, the individuals inside a company must have a clear path to seeing both their strengths and weaknesses. By doing so, the entire organization becomes stronger.

For instance, if you know your team's weaknesses, you'll know precisely how to move forward with your team-building efforts. Because you know your team's needs, you'll look for people who are strong in areas where your team is weak. Your team will then accomplish more than it could otherwise.

Imagine workplaces where entire organizations were built on Trust and Understanding. Not only did I think this was possible, but it also became my mission.

I believe with all my heart that the foundation of success for our business is our focus on Trust and Understanding. And building Trust and Understanding is at the core of all of our professional relationships.

As a result, we invested countless hours showing our team members and clients that we cared for their well-being, and they rewarded us with hard work and loyalty. We realized that our business was only as strong as its individual members. So we worked together to accomplish goals that would benefit everyone. In the following section, I'll use some concepts that I have adapted from Korean culture to explain what this process requires. First, I'll explain how *koraji* is the first ingredient to building Trust and Understanding. After that, I'll provide three additional ingredients that will be key parts of your business.

Koraji: The First Step to Building Trust and Understanding

Koraji, pronounced *core-RAW-gee,* is a Korean word that typically means "to know yourself." When I say, "I know my koraji," it means that I understand myself and who I am. Koraji includes your goals and dreams as well as your strengths and weaknesses. Koraji also extends to those around you. In other words, you know yourself *and* your team members.

When you know your strengths and the strengths of those around you, your team will be stronger. When you identify your weaknesses and the weaknesses of your team members, you'll know exactly where you need to improve. As a result, koraji can change your business and your life, but only if you are ready to accept help from an experienced professional who will act as a **mentor in your business**. A mentor's role is to help you understand your koraji and improve the areas in your life that challenge you. Thus he or she plays a key role within your team. Mentors are a powerful example of why working as a team is better than working on your own.

Four Ingredients for Building Trust and Understanding

Behind every good meal is a recipe. You probably have memories of what happened when a skilled cook prepared the right ingredients: a main dish that you couldn't wait to eat again or a dessert that you told your friends they must eat. Koraji is one of the main ingredients of your recipe for building Trust and Understanding. The complete Trust and Understanding recipe has the following four main ingredients:

1. Koraji
2. Ssagaji
3. Skinship
4. Underwear Stories

1. Koraji: Know Yourself and Those Around You

At the core of koraji is knowing yourself. The benefit of knowing yourself is that once you do this, you'll have the tools to understand others as well. Knowing yourself includes your background and your personality. If you have bad habits that get in the way of your success, thinking about koraji will help you recognize them. Once you know your shortcomings, you'll be able to figure out how to make better decisions. In addition, you must also learn the koraji of your team members and clients because by doing so, you'll be able to anticipate their needs, which will help them (and you) to succeed.

An Example of Koraji

"John, I want to be a millionaire!" Julia told me. She had recently joined our business and looked forward to her new career.

"Do you know what it takes to earn a high income?" I asked her.

"I think that hard work and focus are a good start," she said.

"Sounds good. So how many hours of work did you put into your business this week?" I asked.

Julia started her answer by giving me a series of excuses for not focusing on her business: She had to take her kids to soccer practice, dance rehearsal, and piano lessons; she volunteered at her church; and she had a PTA meeting at her daughter's school.

"But you didn't answer my question," I said.

It was Thursday, and she calculated her work hours for the past 6 days. "Probably 12 hours total," she answered.

"So you spent, on average, 2 hours a day on your business, but you expect to earn a high income. Within a 12-hour workweek, do you think you can cram meetings with team members?

contacting potential referrals, getting information about potential clients, preparing presentations, and doing everything else to build your business?" I asked.

Julia realized how silly she sounded. She wanted to earn a high income, but she was making excuses instead of putting in the effort. Until she and I spoke, Julia hadn't learned her personal koraji, which resulted in wishes (wanting to be a millionaire) that didn't match reality (working an average of 2 hours a day). Up to this point, she didn't understand that to arrive at her goal, she would first have to take a series of important steps. This might sound like an extreme example, but it is amazing how many people don't realize their koraji. In fact, I've had similar conversations many times over the years.

Adults Need Professional Mentors for Koraji

Children regularly learn their koraji from their parents. For example, parents reward kids for good behavior and give consequences and punishments when they misbehave. During our school years, teachers provide knowledge and help us make good choices. Once we reach adulthood and complete our formal education, however, this guidance usually stops. The results are adults who make the same mistakes over and over again. In addition, most adults have no system to improve their lives because no one they trust and respect is there to ask them, "What do you think of the choices you've been making lately?" and "Do you think there are better approaches that you can take?"

In the two examples I gave of how children learn their koraji, you'll notice that they involved parents and teachers. This points to the fact that whether you're a child or an adult, koraji is something you *cannot* learn by yourself. While it certainly takes your own effort for koraji to benefit you, *learning your koraji requires someone else's help.* This is because our **ego** often gets in the way of our ability to accomplish our professional goals. Our ego includes our background and experiences from which we view those around us as well as ourselves. It may cause us to view events differently from how they really are. But if we're able to clearly see how our ego can hold us back, we have recognized one of the biggest obstacles to our professional success. Thus outsiders are the best guide to our strengths and weaknesses because they're not looking at us through our ego.

"But what about husbands, wives, and bosses? Can't they help us learn our koraji?" you may ask. In the case of significant others, our relationship to them is too personal. If a husband or wife points out your shortcomings, it usually creates tension in the personal relationship, and you may not accept his or her advice. In the case of bosses, the nature of the relationship makes you too vulnerable to their personal opinion. Because bosses can fire you, you'll do whatever they say regardless of whether it's in your best interests or whether you really agree with their point of view.

As you can see, learning your koraji and the koraji of others may have seemed simple at first, but it requires more than just thinking about who you are. In our business, we found that the solution to this problem is to match new team members with experienced professionals who serve as **mentors**.

Mentorship Is an Ancient Practice

For centuries, **mentors** have played a central role in moving civilizations forward. They have passed on their wisdom to those with less experience. This giving of wisdom usually required understanding the other person's needs. It also called for the person receiving guidance to remain humble; he or she had to understand that the mentor's role was to point out strengths *and* weaknesses. In other words, mentors helped those within their group to learn their koraji. But mentorship was only effective when a student had an attitude of "I'm willing to put in the effort and do whatever is required to improve myself."

In our modern culture, we've lost this mentor-student relationship, which makes learning your koraji very difficult. This is unfortunate because when we learn our koraji, we can reach our career goals faster than is otherwise possible. Because I understood the power of koraji, I knew that for our business to be successful, koraji would have to be one of the most important parts of our business system. So how would I turn koraji, which was really just an idea, into *a core business value?* The way to do this was to match every new team member with an experienced professional who could be a business mentor.

A mentor's role is to guide you. Meanwhile, you must maintain an open mind. In order for a mentor to be able to help you, he or she will need to know your strengths *and your weaknesses.*

Most importantly, for the relationship to work, both you and your mentor must respect one another. The Korean word *ssagaji* expresses this type of mutual respect. Ssagaji is the second ingredient to building Trust and Understanding.

2. Ssagaji: A New Vision of Respect

Imagine that you're at your favorite restaurant. It's in a strip mall, and from the outside it doesn't look very nice. In fact, most potential customers think that the food will probably not be very good based on the appearance of the restaurant. But you know better. In fact, you've just finished the best cake you've ever eaten. You quickly write down the name of the dessert and can't wait to look up the recipe online. At home, you search "chocolate lava cake." You print out the recipe, you buy all the ingredients, and you follow the directions. Despite all your hard work, the cake tastes nothing like what you had at the restaurant.

When you return to the restaurant, you talk to the chef, who is someone you've known for years. You share how you tried to bake the chocolate lava cake, and he asks you questions. After finding out how you made the cake, he thinks that the oven temperature was too low.

On your way home from the restaurant, your friend calls you. You share how you tried to bake the chocolate lava cake and what the chef told you. "You're going to listen to him?" she asks. She doesn't think the chef's opinion is very valuable because his restaurant isn't nice looking. In her view, the problem has nothing to do with the oven temperature. Instead, you added too much flour to the recipe. But your friend only bakes once in a while.

So whose advice do you follow—the chef with the shabby restaurant or your friend who doesn't bake very often?

Despite how the chef's restaurant looks, you know that it's important to judge a situation based on more than just appearances. You realize that the chef is an expert dessert maker, and you've eaten his creations many, many times. Because of these facts, you follow his advice. Similarly, when you're in a new industry and career, you need a mentor whom you trust and respect. In our organization, we use the Korean word *ssagaji* to describe this type of respect.

Ssagaji, pronounced *saw-GAW-gee*, means respect for another person or institution. Although respect may seem like a simple idea, it's not the same everywhere.

In its original form, the concept of ssagaji is based on Asian cultures that have been heavily influenced by ancient China. Most people in nations like China, Korea, and Japan hold a similar understanding of what respect means. In those countries, people regularly give respect to others based on their age, their profession, and their rank in life.

On the other hand, cultures influenced by Western Europe often have a different view of respect. A person's age does not always determine the respect we give him or her. In the United States, for example, we may give *more* respect to a 25-year-old CEO of a successful Internet business than we would to a 55-year-old engineer who is working for that CEO. In addition, we frequently give respect to people based on their income and their college degrees.

Our Business Ssagaji Is a Mix of East and West

In our business, we've stripped ssagaji of its cultural limitations. We have homemakers mentoring young adults and young adults teaching people old enough to be their parents. This is possible because we've taken the best parts of respect from Eastern and Western cultures and have incorporated them into our business principles. In our business, respect is not just about the mentor's age, his or her income, or where he or she attended college. Rather, respect is about a mentor's business experience and the time he or she will spend to support you. But respect must be mutual. Thus it extends to you as well. Both you and your mentor must maintain mutual respect in order for your professional relationship to work.

Ssagaji in our business means to be humble, trusting, and willing to put in the effort to improve your life and business. Your mentor will help you learn your koraji, and his or her feedback will be both positive and negative. Your mentor will point out your successes and tell you what you're doing right. Meanwhile, when you're struggling, your mentor will let you know where you need to improve. Unfortunately, if you're closed-minded and unwilling to learn, you'll refuse to accept his or her advice. And if you're not trusting, your mentor's guidance won't help you.

3. Developing Ssagaji Through Skinship

Previously, I shared that in our business, we match new team members with business mentors. The goal is that through these connections, everyone will learn his or her own koraji as well as the koraji of others. Furthermore, for a mentor to truly be able to help you, ssagaji must be at the center of your relationship with him or her. Deepening ssagaji takes commitment and time. In our business, we develop ssagaji through what we call skinship.

The word *skinship* comes from words such as *friendship* and *kinship*, which is the connection between people who are related to each other. Add the word *skin* and you have *skinship*. It was originally used in Japan as a way to describe a mother's connection to a child. It also has to do with being naked, not in the sense of not wearing any clothes, but in the sense of being emotionally open to another person. In either case, this "nakedness" can be very uncomfortable.

Many of us in the United States have been raised to value our independence and our personal privacy. Sayings like "It's none of your business" express how important privacy is. But just a couple of generations ago in this country, such ideas about privacy weren't common. For example, the dividing line between one family's property and another's was often difficult to figure out—one backyard connected to another. In today's suburbs, we have fences and thick walls separating us from the houses next to us. The popular saying "Tall fences make good neighbors" describes how many of us feel that detachment from those close to us is a desirable quality. In addition, most of us value not only the spaces in which we live, but our personal space as well, which is the distance between us and the person next to us. But the idea of personal space is not the same everywhere.

In countries like South Korea and Japan, millions of people are packed into huge cities. Men and women are used to tight quarters in subways, on busy streets, and in small apartments and homes. What may be viewed as an invasion of "my personal space" for someone in the U.S. may seem very normal for someone who grew up in either of these countries.

In order to build Trust and Understanding, I realized that people within our business needed to break down the personal and emotional space that would keep them from learning their koraji and developing ssagaji. Otherwise, Trust and Understanding would be nothing more than a slogan or a corporate saying—a belief system that we repeated to each other but in reality didn't take seriously. That's one of the biggest problems with many companies in the U.S. today.

Many other businesses may say that caring is built into their corporate culture, that leaders understand their team members, and that team members trust their leaders, but we know that this isn't always the case. No one trusts anyone within most companies because most leaders and employees are only looking out for themselves. This selfish mindset exists mainly because everyone is bouncing back and forth between fear and desire: *fear of getting fired* and *desire to get promoted*.

But imagine a different type of business. What if your success depended on the success of others? What if taking the self-centered approach actually guaranteed failure? The system of building Trust and Understanding works for us because in our business, you succeed only when your team members do as well.

Skinship Is Part of Our Business

As I shared earlier, skinship isn't about being physically naked—I'm sure that many of you are relieved to read that! Instead, skinship is what will turn ssagaji into something deeper that applies to you and your mentor. It requires spending time to learn about the other person. It also means that you and your mentor are emotionally open to each other. Let me give you an example of what I mean.

Imagine that you are on a first date with a person. The moment you meet at the restaurant, the other person pulls out a ring and asks, "Will you marry me?"

I think you'd agree that this is not the best way to develop a deep relationship. In fact, most of us would probably leave the restaurant as fast as we could. But let's take this story a step further. Imagine that you decided to accept the proposal. Soon after, you're walking down the aisle with your new spouse. What would most likely be the outcome of this marriage, which merged two strangers? Probably divorce. Jumping into any commitment too quickly—whether it's romantic, business, or financial—usually ends badly.

Thus skinship shouldn't be rushed. It takes time and commitment, but that doesn't mean it's complicated. Skinship could be as simple as grabbing a coffee at Starbucks, or it could be as intimate as visiting your mentor's home and getting to know his or her family. Just as there's not just one way to make a friendship work, there are several methods to practicing skinship.

Skinship Is an Equal Exchange

Healthy marriages require a mutual exchange of communication. Likewise, effective skinship involves two-way openness. Through spending time together, you and your mentor are learning about each other's lives and sharing about one another's strengths and weaknesses as well, all of which, in the end, build Trust and Understanding.

Developing true ssagaji requires that both you and your mentor know details about each other that reach beyond the typical boundaries that we create. This includes more than just the facts that would appear on a resume, such as your education, work experience, and career accomplishments. Although this information is helpful, it's just a first step.

Skinship runs far deeper. It involves you and your mentor's personal and professional histories, the difficult situations you've experienced, and how you have overcome or are still working on overcoming them. This knowledge of one another's backgrounds builds trust that is more than just a corporate slogan in a brochure—one that nobody really cares about. It's an understanding that you and your mentor will depend on one another's koraji to accomplish goals that will benefit both of you.

Practicing skinship is what speeds up ssagaji. As a result, koraji deepens as well. When entire teams apply the principles of koraji, ssagaji, and skinship, the results are amazing. Teams accomplish goals faster than otherwise possible. Communication improves, and team members have a clear understanding of what they're supposed to accomplish. When setbacks arise, as they always do, teams overcome them quickly and move on.

You might be a bit afraid that developing skinship will take a long time. One way to speed up the process of skinship is by sharing your **underwear stories**.

4. Underwear Stories: The Direct Route to Skinship

For many of us who were raised in this country, we were taught to keep conversations light and carefree. We are often told things such as "Mind your own business" and "Never talk about politics, religion, sex, or money." We respond to a "How you doing?" with an automatic "fine," "good," or something equally harmless—even if we're feeling suicidal or happy beyond belief. Imagine if you asked a coworker, "How are you today?" and he responded with "Terrible. I'm so depressed because of the fight I had with my wife this morning, and I'm tired of my kids." Such an honest answer would probably leave you not knowing what to say next.

The underwear story takes the relationship between you and your mentor beyond the culturally accepted ways that most relationships work. Through sharing your underwear stories, you can quickly build a level of Trust and Understanding that is completely absent in today's companies.

An underwear story has four features:

1. It's about you.
2. It provides a deep insight into one or more aspects of your personality.
3. It deepens Trust and Understanding between you and the listener.
4. It builds your self-confidence.

Storytelling is a way that humans have shared information with each other for tens of thousands of years. Sharing stories with one another is a powerful way that humans connect with each other. It's how we learn about one another and help each other in ways that we can't predict. In fact, you never know how your underwear story will help someone else. By knowing someone's past struggles, you'll be able to identify if he or she is repeating bad habits in the present. For instance, you may share how difficult life became when your parents divorced, and your mentor will know exactly how you feel. Or your mentor may talk about how he and his dad spent a month building a car together and how meaningful that was to him. Both examples show how the stories we share have the ability to build trust and deepen understanding of one another.

Underwear stories can be triumphant or heartbreaking. They can cover several years of your life, or they can describe one moment. You can have short underwear stories that you share on a regular basis, or you can have long ones that you save for once in a while. You can tell your underwear story casually to one person, or it can be done more formally, such as in a prepared presentation in front of an audience.

If your underwear story is about a proud event in your life, you will probably be happy to share it. But if it's about something painful, it may be difficult to talk about. Through your underwear stories, you and your mentor are learning about each other's koraji. Both of you should listen without judgment and respect the other person's story as if it were your own.

Underwear stories also build your self-confidence. For example, a story of overcoming a difficult situation reminds you of your inner strength. You remember that you have the ability to improve your life. In this regard, underwear stories boost your self-confidence *and* the self-confidence of those who will learn from your experience.

My Underwear Story

In order to help you understand more about underwear stories, I'll share a personal experience.

When I arrived in the United States, I was 25 years old. About three years later, I was hired at an auto parts store. My English was not very good, so my boss had me keep track of inventory, which wouldn't require me to talk to customers very much. Every day, I showed up at the warehouse and counted parts. For many, this work would seem very boring.

I'm by nature a very curious and observant person, and I

quickly began noticing that the inventory system had serious problems. For instance, parts would come in, and there was no consistent way to keep track of their arrival. So nearly half the parts weren't even in the inventory system. But because the day-to-day work was so demanding, I didn't have enough time to actually fix how we took inventory. The only way to solve the problem was to spend extra time at the warehouse.

Once my shift was over, I'd go home and eat dinner. Then I'd return to work when no one else was around. I'd gather the auto parts manual—which became my work bible—and for hours I'd study all the parts in the warehouse. Within months, I had memorized the warehouse's entire inventory. It wasn't as if I had a special gift for memorization. Instead, it was through what's called "drill and kill": Just as we memorize multiplication in elementary school through doing math problems over and over again, I memorized the inventory by reviewing parts countless times. I'd show up at work in the morning and keep track of what parts went in and out. After work, I'd study all the different parts we had in stock. Eventually, my coworkers started noticing.

I recall how a customer came into the store and asked for a part. "Do you have an engine starter for a 1980 Chevrolet Monte Carlo?" he asked.

The sales rep went to the warehouse and couldn't find one.

"No, I'm sorry—we're out," he said when he came back. I was working nearby and overheard the conversation.

"Actually, we have two," I said. I went to the warehouse and brought the part back.

This began to happen repeatedly. Customers who would have left the store without their part and who probably would have bought one from a competitor were now buying from us. Sales reps started relying on me instead of the inventory system. I'd quickly let them know whether or not a part was in stock, and more often than not, the answer was "Yes, we have it."

Sales reps saw their sales volume and commissions increase. During those months, I didn't have to pay for my own lunch very often because my coworkers would show their gratitude by buying my meals. Then the owner began noticing as well. Not only did he see how the sales reps counted on my knowledge of the store inventory, but he also saw how his profits had increased since he'd hired me. The biggest reward for the extra hours I put in every day came when the owner asked me to meet with him.

"Would you like to be the store manager?" he asked.

I couldn't believe that he was asking me such a question. I hadn't even been there for a year, so this was the last thing I ever thought he'd ask me. But I had to be honest. "Sir, my English isn't very good," I said.

"You think I didn't know that already?" he joked. He couldn't have cared less about my poor language skills. What he recognized was my determination, my respect for the business, and how all of this had increased the store's profits.

Breaking Down My Underwear Story

Overall, this example clearly shows the key parts of a good underwear story: It's about me, it helps you learn my koraji, it builds Trust and Understanding because you learn something personal about me, and it gives me confidence because it reminds me of my ability to overcome difficult situations.

As you can see, it's not a story about my entire life. Rather, this underwear story spans a couple of months. I could certainly make it much longer by adding details. But from this short underwear story, you gain insight into my personality: I'm very curious and determined to solve problems when I find them. It provides background about my life: I'm from South Korea, and I arrived in the U.S. speaking very little English. Because an underwear story is often shared in casual conversation, your mentor will probably ask you questions, so it will become more of a conversation than a speech. But if you were sharing your underwear story during a team meeting, it could certainly sound like a presentation that you prepared ahead of time.

By reading my story, I hope you can relate to my experiences. Perhaps you're an immigrant to the United States, or someone close to you is. Maybe you started at the very bottom in a job and worked your way up. Perhaps you can understand how I found a problem and did whatever it took to solve it. Or maybe you wish you were more focused and would like to learn from me. Whatever the case, it is through underwear stories that we build skinship, begin to understand each other, and establish mutual respect, which we need for our business relationship.

Now that you understand the key ingredients of our business, you're ready to learn about the mindset and system you'll need. In the next chapter, I'll describe the importance of having an ownership mentality and how following a business system can save you time and effort.

Chapter 2

The Importance of a Mindset and System

In the previous chapter, I shared my **underwear story**. If you recall, every underwear story has four parts: It's about you, it provides a deep insight into one or more aspects of your personality, it deepens Trust and Understanding between you and the listener, and it builds your self-confidence.

Shortly after I was hired as an entry-level employee in the auto parts store, I realized that the business's inventory system was in need of serious help. So after a long day's work, I would return to the warehouse in order to account for all the parts that weren't properly recorded. Meanwhile, I wasn't getting paid to spend the extra time memorizing the warehouse's inventory, and no one was rewarding me for my efforts.

So what motivated me to return to the warehouse when I could have stayed home and relaxed instead? At the time, if you had asked what my reasons were, I probably would have told you that I liked the challenge of learning new things and solving problems. But when I look back on the experience through the eyes of a successful businessperson, I realize that I had an **ownership mentality**—even though I was a worker starting at the very bottom. In this chapter, I'll explain what I mean by "ownership mentality" and how it's drastically different from a "worker mentality."

You Need an Ownership Mentality for True Success

Imagine that you own a Chinese restaurant. Let's call it the Chop Chop Café. You have a staff of employees: a cook, two servers, a busboy, and a host.

It's 7:00 a.m. on Monday and, as always, you're the first to arrive at the restaurant. Shortly after, a truck comes to drop off your daily food delivery. The deliveryman carries several large boxes into your kitchen. When he has you sign off on the delivery, he shares the bad news: no rice today.

"You know how important rice is to my restaurant. How can you tell me that you don't have any?" you ask.

He apologizes, but there wasn't any in the warehouse that morning. Both of you realize that there's nothing the deliveryman can do to fix the problem. Once he leaves, you spend the next two hours driving to several grocery stores and buying bags and bags of the type of rice that your customers expect you to serve them.

At 4:00 p.m., an hour before you open for dinner, one of your servers calls you. "Boss, I have the flu, and I can't make it today," he says. You accept that you can't force him to come to work. It will now be you and the other server taking orders all evening.

At 7:00 o'clock, your tables are full of guests. The cook is preparing plates as fast as you and the other server can carry them to customers. The phone rings. It's the basketball coach of your cook's daughter. His teenager injured herself at practice and is on her way to the hospital. You throw on an apron and let the cook meet his daughter in the emergency room.

It's 12:00 midnight when you turn off the restaurant lights and lock the door behind you. From the time you arrived at work in the morning till the last dish was washed, it's been one of the longest days you've had in recent memory. Running a business isn't easy, especially when your staff doesn't share the same level of motivation that you do.

Clearly, most restaurants don't experience all of the problems in one evening that I described. But the example points to the major difference between the ownership mentality and the worker mentality.

Worker Mentality: The deliveryman had the option to tell you he had no rice, the server knew he could call in sick, and the cook assumed he could leave the restaurant early because you could take over. They did not feel the direct effect of their actions on the restaurant in the same way that you, the restaurant owner, would.

When the deliveryman arrived with no rice, his worker mentality explained why he *didn't* say, "I'll spend the next two hours driving around to find and deliver the brand of rice that you need." He didn't see the connection between *not delivering* rice and you *not being able* to run your restaurant properly.

Ownership Mentality: Meanwhile, as a restaurant owner, you know that your customers count on you to prepare food that they have come to expect. If they ordered rice, they probably wouldn't accept the excuse, "Sorry, we have no rice because the deliveryman didn't bring any today." And they wouldn't accept other excuses such as, "I apologize that your food is cold and late. The reason is that my server called in sick." Instead, if you didn't meet their expectations, they might never come back again.

In addition, if you had the flu, you could decide to stay home and rest. But unlike the server who called in sick, you wouldn't be able to just focus on yourself as you were trying to get better. Instead, you'd be wondering how the restaurant was doing without you there. Was the host properly seating guests? Was the food being prepared to your standards? Were the servers following the script that you had practiced with them countless times?

I believe that the lack of an ownership mentality explains why so many first businesses fail—and I'm talking about *all types of businesses,* not just restaurants. When problems arise, business owners who have a worker mentality often give up too quickly and don't do everything necessary to succeed.

Breaking Out of the Boxed Life

So if the ownership mentality requires so much responsibility, why would anyone want it? To answer this question, let's first look at the limitations of the worker mentality. The worker mentality is rooted in what I call a **boxed life**. A box is something that has a bottom, sides, and a top, and its job is to contain something within its walls. When you fill a box, you hope that it will hold whatever is inside. I'm certain that all of us have experienced what happens when a box falls apart—its contents spill out.

When I say, "boxed life," I'm comparing our lives to a box. Those with a worker mentality need to be held within set rules—think of these as the container. They need someone to tell them where to show up to work from Monday to Friday, what time to arrive, what time to eat lunch, and what time to leave. They need their bosses to tell them how to fill their work hours. Those with a worker mentality can become so dependent on the rules of the boxed life that when they're left to make their own decisions, they have no idea what to do.

Once people living a boxed life are done with their jobs, they socialize with friends, take care of their families, go to sleep, and start over the next day. While routines such as these are very important, they can be harmful if they're keeping you from growing and challenging yourself. A boxed life can keep you from achieving bigger things in your career. In contrast, an ownership mentality gives you freedom and control over your success.

Everyone Should Have an Ownership Mentality

The goals of the owner and those of the worker are often in conflict. Owners realize that regardless of the obstacles that get in their way, such as wrong food deliveries and employees who don't show up, the restaurant doors must remain open no matter what, and the meals must be served exactly as customers expect. Otherwise, the owners' businesses will fail.

Here's where the restaurant example has its limitations. In the restaurant business, one person with an ownership mentality can run a successful business employing a team of individuals who all have a worker mentality. In this case, it's "you versus your employees." You're the only one who realizes or cares that the future of the restaurant depends on the strength of your entire staff. Meanwhile, the employees are mainly just concerned about themselves. Their effort is based either on a fear of getting fired or a desire to get promoted. As a result, your employees won't invest the same energy that you would. But in our business, this formula will not work. Allow me to illustrate my point.

Imagine that you're organizing a very important meeting. Attending will be people, like you, who are growing their businesses as well as clients and potential clients. Out of all these people, you're the only one with an ownership mentality, which explains why you made sure that the chairs were arranged properly, the lights were on, and the refreshments were prepared before anyone else arrived.

It's time to start the meeting, and the speaker is standing in front of the audience. She says her first word. Unfortunately, no one can hear her because the microphone isn't working. But because everyone except you has a worker mentality, they all remain in their seats and wait for *someone else* to fix the problem. In other words, their boxed lives keep them from taking action. Meanwhile, those who are attending the meeting for the first time have no idea what's going on. As always, you take charge of the situation. You walk up to the microphone and realize that it's broken. You quickly replace it with another, and the meeting continues.

In a team setting, if your team members all have a worker mentality, you'll find yourself spending countless hours trying to help people who really don't care about your business. You'll be constantly checking on them to make sure they complete the most basic tasks and will wonder why they can't solve problems on their own. In other words, your time is spent trying to make up for those with a worker mentality.

In the end, you'll find yourself exhausted, frustrated, and with poor outcomes. I know because I have seen this throughout my career. I eventually realized that when I surrounded myself with those who had an ownership mentality and we all shared Trust and Understanding, we did better than if I tried to do everything myself. Therefore, when I started my business, I made sure that my team members understood the importance of Trust and Understanding and the difference between a worker and an ownership mentality.

Upgrade Your "Software": How to Improve Your Mentality

Whether you currently have a worker or an ownership mentality, you can always improve yourself. But in order to upgrade your "software" (your skills and mindset), you must ask yourself, "At the deepest core of my being, am I willing to do what it takes to make my situation better?"

In addition, if you're stuck in a way of thinking that you know isn't good for you, you've already taken an important step. Because you're aware of your weaknesses and limitations, you can now determine what you need to do differently. For instance, if you have a worker mentality, you can tell yourself that you will think and act as if you had an ownership mentality, no matter what. Here's where a mentor plays an important role by being your guide.

Upgrading your software is something that you should constantly do, even if you already have an ownership mentality. In fact, success should never stop you from growing. You must regularly ask yourself, "Am I doing everything possible to live up to what it means to have an ownership mentality?"

I've worked with team members who clearly seemed to have an ownership mentality. As expected, they performed to a high level, and their businesses grew quickly. Unfortunately, their ownership mentality had its limits. Once they accomplished a certain degree of success, they stopped opening their minds to new ideas. They didn't continue to set new goals and overcome new challenges. They only did the things that were comfortable and that they were used to doing. Over time, their momentum slowed, and they couldn't figure out why.

True Success Requires an Ownership Mentality *and* Trust and Understanding

In our business, teamwork is the key to meeting common goals. By combining everyone's strengths, the entire team benefits. For instance, let's say that you have two salespeople. Sally has superior product knowledge, while David has amazing people skills. But because they don't work together, both have trouble succeeding.

Sally struggles to schedule appointments and doesn't know how to talk to clients. Meanwhile, David meets plenty of people, but he has a difficult time answering detailed questions about products. In the end, neither of them sells much. Even if both have an ownership mentality, they haven't developed Trust and Understanding.

Now imagine that both Sally and David want to do well, and they realize they will both accomplish their goals faster if they work together. They decide to combine their strengths. David sets up lots of appointments for both of them. During meetings, Sally is able to answer difficult questions. As a result of working together, they quickly turn their prospects into clients.

Follow a System for Success

Once you have a team in which all of you have the same ownership mentality and there is Trust and Understanding between the members, you need systems and procedures to make sure your business runs efficiently and will be able to grow. Otherwise, you'll be wasting lots of time repeating tasks that someone else already took care of, not completing tasks that you thought someone else already took care of, clearing up miscommunication, and neglecting to meet your clients' needs.

Let's go back to our Chop Chop Café example. The most popular item on your menu is the Chop Chop Salad, which has your secret dressing. People talk about your special salad on restaurant blogs, they order it for their office parties, and they buy it for friends. It even won "Best Salad" in the local newspaper's annual food issue. Because of the success of your first restaurant, you decide to open a second Chop Chop Café. You use the same menu that made your first restaurant popular. Within months after opening Chop Chop Café #2, it becomes a profitable restaurant.

It's been years since you took a vacation. Because you believe your staff knows how to run the restaurant without you, you finally decide to go on a well-deserved trip. When you return, you look over the receipts and see that sales decreased by 40 percent while you were away. Not only that, but the most popular item at Chop Chop Café #1, which is the award-winning Chop Chop Salad, is hardly ordered at your new restaurant. You start asking your customers why they aren't ordering the special salad at Café #2.

"It doesn't taste the same" is the most common answer.

You taste the dressing for yourself. Your customers are right!

As a result, you investigate. You eventually see that there are new items on your food order list that you don't recognize. You ask your cook about this.

"Why are we ordering different brands of soy sauce, oil, and vinegar than we did before?" you ask.

"I was looking to cut costs, so I switched over to cheaper brands for the food we buy," he says. Part of you appreciates that he was doing his best to save the restaurant money. At the same time, moving away from the exact ingredients that made the Chop Chop Salad successful has hurt your profits.

Don't Reinvent the Wheel

Sayings like this were invented to express the mistake that your chef made while you were on vacation. Another common expression is "If it ain't broke, don't fix it!" You created a successful system, and you trained others to follow it. The system broke down when the chef stopped following the recipe, and as a result, your business suffered.

Mistakes like this can be both **unintentional** (accidental) and **intentional** (on purpose). Your chef's mistake is an example of an **intentional** error. He thought he was doing you a favor by saving you money. But his decision to change the system hurt your business.

There are many examples of **unintentional** errors. For instance, you could have trained your chefs to cook food incorrectly, or you could have become too busy with paperwork, and as a result, your team members stopped following your customer service system.

In both examples, you had a system in place. Although you initially trained your team to follow it, they stopped sticking to it. Whether the changes they made were big or small, in the end, a breakdown in your system hurt your business.

I'm not against new ideas, doing things differently, and thinking "outside the boxed life." In fact, much of what you've read so far is about a new way of thinking about business. Furthermore, creating Trust and Understanding is a new concept for many, and it's a "wheel worth reinventing." But for you to learn the elements of building Trust and Understanding, such as koraji, ssagaji, and skinship, requires a tremendous time investment. Add to that the daily tasks of scheduling meetings, conducting presentations, coordinating team members, and more, and you will not have time to watch over every single thing your team does. Thus when there is a proven system in place, such as the one we have in our business, you and your team members must place trust in that system. If you don't, you'll end up with a business that is unmanageable because of the countless intentional and unintentional mistakes that you'll have to fix.

So far, you've learned the ingredients of how to succeed in our business. In this chapter, I described the importance of an ownership mentality, and I also explained how your continued success requires you and your team members to follow a system. Now that you understand the fundamentals, you're ready for the next step. In the following chapter, I'll provide a checklist that will help you decide whether our business is for you.

Chapter 3

The Green Button Checklist

When I started in this business, I made countless mistakes, both big and small. I have plenty of underwear stories to prove my point! Over the years, I learned that some errors were bigger than others. In fact, I recognized that you can recover from certain mistakes quickly, while others may cause your business to fail.

As our business grew, I learned how to teach team members how they could be successful. I helped them avoid making the mistakes that I did. I also learned to identify the qualities people needed in order to succeed. In this chapter, I'll help you determine whether you're ready to experience success in our business.

Am I Ready for Business?

Before you "press the green button"—which is how we describe your decision to move forward—and spend time and energy building your team, it's important to make sure that this business is right for you. I've developed seven key questions to guide you. These have developed from years of career experience. They express how this business can affect your life. In the end, people who have trouble answering these questions may want to focus their energy somewhere else. The Green Button Checklist is another example that illustrates Trust and Understanding. We care about your success. Thus we want you to know, before you start, whether this business is for you.

After each question, I'll provide what you need to think about as you consider your answers. Be as honest as possible and answer all of them. *I strongly recommend that you go over these questions with your potential business mentor.* Even if the results aren't what you had hoped for, being truthful will save you lots of time and trouble.

1. What are your goals, and what's your level of commitment to fulfilling your goals?

I call this the "reality check question." It includes the following sub-questions:

    a. How much money do you want to earn?

    b. How hard are you willing to work to reach your income goals?

    c. Do your answers to "a" and "b" match?

Let's say your answer to sub-question a is "I want to earn $1,000,000 a year." And your answer to sub-question b is "I want to work ten hours a week." Combined, these two answers will guarantee failure. Our business isn't a get-rich-quick scheme. In this example, you're going to have to work harder or earn a lot less—especially at the beginning, when your time investment will be high and your income will be low.

2. Are you a team player?

This is the teamwork question. It first involves asking yourself, "Am I willing to be mentored by someone else?"

Being mentored requires putting aside your ego and accepting advice and training. You'll be trained by your mentor, and in order for the relationship to work, you must have respect for each other. In addition, you're going to collaborate with people of different ages, ethnicities, and backgrounds, and respect must be at the core of everyone's relationship to one another.

Next, teamwork involves your ability to give back and your willingness to focus on your entire team's interests above your own. Think of your business as a baseball team. Imagine that you're one of the pitchers, and your coach tells you that you'll sit out the next game so that you can rest. Do you support your team by showing up to the game, even though you know you won't pitch that day? Or do you stay home because attending won't benefit you? The answer, from our point of view, is that you show up to the game.

3. Ownership or worker—what kind of mentality do you have?

In Chapter 2: The Importance of a Mindset and System, I explain the difference between the two mentalities. Be sure you understand both and recognize that they can change. For example, with enough time and effort, a worker mentality can be upgraded to an ownership mentality. In the end, success in our business requires an ownership mentality.

4. What is your "why"?

Why are you in this business? This question has to do with how motivated you are to succeed. There are three typical types of motivations:

1. Strong motivation
2. Weak motivation
3. Somewhere in between

I'll illustrate the first two by providing extreme examples in order to make my point as clear as possible.

Strong Motivation

Overcoming difficulties is one of the biggest reasons that most of us are willing to make changes in our lives. And often the bigger the pain, the more motivated we are to change. For example, let's say that you're a father who supports his wife and two young children. You have monthly bills and a mortgage, and you're about to be laid off due to corporate downsizing.

You never finished college, which limits your career options. You join our business because you see an opportunity to support your family and have a fulfilling career. But because your family depends on you, failure is not an option. You realize that while others may be smarter and more talented than you, no one will work harder. Thus you'll follow your mentor's advice and do whatever it takes to succeed.

Weak Motivation

Imagine that you have a stable full-time job. You have a Master's in Business Administration (MBA), you have extensive knowledge of the financial services industry, you have some savings, and you're a hard worker. You decide to join our business because you like the idea of earning additional money every year. But if you don't earn anything extra, your life will be fine. When compared to the father who will lose his job, you're in a far better place. But your strengths can also become weaknesses. Our business requires tremendous dedication. So will it be worth the hours you need to invest in your business? And will it be worth taking on the stress and challenges for perhaps only a small reward (additional income)? Maybe . . . but someone with a stronger motivation will probably put forth more effort to succeed.

Somewhere In Between

Your family's future may not depend on whether or not you succeed in our business. At the same time, your circumstances may not be so great that you can take our business lightly.

Although it's helpful to have a strong motivation, a weak one won't keep you from succeeding. Regardless of whether your motivation is strong, weak, or somewhere in between, your commitment level must be high. This is because each of the ingredients for creating Trust and Understanding—koraji, ssagaji, and skinship—requires a large investment of time.

In addition, whatever your motivation is, your ability to talk about your "why" is very important in our business. The "why" explains "why you decided to do this business," and the stronger your "why," the better. In fact, your "why" is key to your success. In the example of the strong and weak motivations, the person with the weak motivation had more education and money. Although he or she had a better background, the person with the stronger motivation had a more powerful "why," and this is what will keep him motivated when facing difficult situations. For instance, if both have to deal with a major obstacle, the one with the weaker motivation will be more likely to say, "I give up!" while the one with the stronger motivation will say, "I'll do whatever it takes to find a solution."

Your "why" is also a powerful tool to introduce new team members to your business. In this way, your "why" is also an underwear story. When others can relate to your reasons for joining our business, such as the difficult circumstances you have faced and the ways in which you want to improve your life, they may also see how their lives can improve. Whether you're talking to a potential client or team member, the stronger and more powerful your underwear story, the easier it is for others to relate to you.

In fact, many people were motivated to join my team after hearing my underwear story. They thought, "If John can achieve his dreams, I can, too!" They were inspired by my story, they were able to relate to my experiences, and they believed that I'd be a great person to work with.

5. What is your career and financial status?

Most of us will fall under one of three common scenarios:

1. I don't have a job.
2. I have a well-paying job.
3. I have a job, but I'm looking for something better.

When you start this business, you will probably have to learn about a number of things, such as financial products, how to be a team member, how to recruit others for your team, how to build ssagaji with your mentor, and much more. You want to take an honest look at your financial situation and ask yourself, "Do I have the time to do this?" The financial industry offers immense career opportunities, but the time investment will also affect your life and the lives of those closest to you.

If you presently have no job, no place to live, and no car, your circumstances may be too difficult to be able to do everything required to join our business. For example, how will you make client appointments if you don't have a car?

Or you may already have a well-paying job that supports your spouse and children. Therefore, it may not make sense to quit your job and start working in our business. Because you won't earn money right away, how will you support your family in the meantime?

Or you may have a job, but you're eager to set your own hours, be your own boss, and be rewarded based on your efforts rather than office politics. In addition, you can afford to support yourself even if you experience a temporary decrease in income. Many people who join our business left jobs in corporate America because they were so unhappy. They complained that they couldn't get promoted because several people were ahead of them in the promotion line. It didn't matter how hard they worked, there was no real future at their jobs. As a result, they were willing and could afford to give up the safety of a paycheck for the possibility of earning more money and having new opportunities to advance in their careers.

6. Do you have a spouse or partner?

If the answer is no, skip this question. If your answer is yes, now ask yourself, "Will he or she support me in a different career?"

If the answer is no, you'll most likely *not* succeed in our business; it's hard enough to do well, even if your answer is "Yes! My spouse will support me 100 percent," let alone if he or she doesn't encourage you in your new venture.

If you've answered, "Yes, my spouse will support me," continue to question 7.

7. How much do you care about others?

No doubt about it, in our business, you have opportunities to earn money—and we hope lots of it. Nevertheless, making money shouldn't be the only reason you join our business. You must also have a genuine interest in improving others' lives. These people include your prospects, clients, and team members. We've built a business based on Trust and Understanding, and the care you have for others is a key to upholding Trust and Understanding.

If money were the only motivation behind becoming part of our business, you would most likely struggle to follow our system. After all, what's the point of building skinship, koraji, and ssagaji if earning money is your sole professional goal? Why not just sell something as soon as possible for as much as possible? Why would you extend help to your team members during times when you may not immediately benefit from the support you provide? Our system is about spending the extra time required to building lasting business relationships. This is not the right system for people who only want shortcuts to making money.

Weighing the Advantages and Disadvantages

Succeeding in business can be one of the most life-changing experiences a person can ever have. But like anything worth having life, success takes hard work and dedication. By going through these six questions, you have taken a significant step in deciding whether this career is for you.

For example, you may have read this chapter and thought to yourself, "I can't afford to do this" or "I don't have an ownership mentality, and I don't think I can develop one" or "My spouse is totally against this." If your answers to the questions have meant that our business isn't a good fit, you've saved some future heartache. If you truly feel that you cannot overcome these obstacles, we understand and appreciate your honesty and your decision.

If, however, your answers have shown that our business is for you, you're ready to push the green button and learn the specific steps of our business system. So far, you've learned the ingredients of our business. In Part 2 of this book, I'll give you the tools to start cooking. The following section will give you the essentials. Our system is called **Basic Training**.

Part 2

Basic Training

CHAPTER 4

An Introduction to Basic Training

I love seeing how our business has improved the lives of countless people. The principles of Trust and Understanding are completely changing the way that motivated people just like you conduct business and serve their clients.

But if you were to ask me if I had any career regrets, I'd say that it took me far too long to realize the importance of team building and how the best teams are based on Trust and Understanding. In fact, I wasted years of my professional life trying to do everything on my own. Early in my career, I failed to figure out what the saying "strength in numbers" meant to my business. In other words, it's far more powerful to work with others than by yourself.

Once I figured out the importance of teamwork and the best way to build a team, I rapidly accomplished more in three years than I had during the previous ten years of my career. The **Basic Training** section that you're reading now is the result of what I learned. By putting this system to work in your business, you'll save yourself lots of time and avoid the mistakes that I made at the beginning of my career.

Basic Training is another way that our business is different from most of the industry. In the following chapters, you'll learn Basic Training's key parts and how to make it work for you. Remember that Basic Training is designed with *you and your business mentor* in mind. In fact, mentorship is what makes Basic Training such a powerful way to launch your career. If you're reading these words without a business mentor, you may find yourself confused and without anyone to answer your questions. Therefore, I strongly advise that you *only follow the Basic Training system with a business mentor's support.*

Also, the focus of Basic Training is to make Trust and Understanding the foundation of how you work. Thus it isn't about providing you product knowledge or sales skills. This may sound odd, considering that you need to know about products to serve your clients. But there are countless books that will teach you about financial products and sales skills. This section has a different purpose.

Basic Training gives you something far more important, which is our **team-building system**. It's what makes our organization special and separates us from others in the industry. By working with a business mentor and putting our system into practice, you'll be able to grow your team and achieve long-term success.

Basic Training Strengths

In the previous chapter, you completed the Green Button Checklist. As a result, you are ready for the next step: Basic Training. When you work closely with your mentor, our approach is designed to help provide the following benefits:

1. **Lower turnover**—Avoid the headaches of having team members constantly join and then quickly leave.
2. **Higher loyalty**—Our organization cares about its team members and clients. We show it through our "relationships first" approach.
3. **Proven results**—Basic Training is quickly learned and quickly repeated, and it leads to your independence.
4. **Long-term success**—Basic Training is designed for those who are serious about being part of an organization for years and years.

Basic Training Organization

Basic Training is focused on specific steps and tasks to complete to get started in this business. I'll explain the Basic Training principles in a particular order, but the actual pattern in which you follow the steps in practice won't always be the same. Just as you'll meet many different types of people in the same. Just as you'll meet many different types of people in our business, there are many different ways to approach them. Your business mentor will be your guide; he or she may make suggestions that don't follow the same order as the following chapters. It's important to learn the principles and then to be flexible as you apply them to your business.

As you read these pages, you may find some of my instructions to be different from how you've learned to build a team and client base. Or you may believe that you have better solutions. But rest assured that all the principles have been tested and are a result of trial and error. So when in doubt, follow the system. Trust me on this. You'll avoid headaches, wasted time, and missed opportunities. Remind yourself that this business requires a new mindset, so expect to be confused sometimes and even hesitant to put what you read into practice.

Basic Training Basics

Throughout the next section, you'll be presented with terms and concepts that are unique or specific to our business. We use these not only in this book but also every day while working with you. And you'll eventually use these terms and concepts when you talk to others in our business. Many of these ideas may seem familiar to you already, so you may find yourself wondering, "Why is John taking time to explain something that's so obvious?"

For instance, in the next section you'll learn about a Home Visit. Although the words *home* and *visit* seem as though they don't require additional explanation to anyone who speaks basic English, for us a Home Visit is not as simple as it seems. In order to have a successful Home Visit, you must follow specific steps that require a lot of preparation. And in the Home Visit chapter, you'll learn what these steps are. So when you're introduced to a term or concept that you think you already know, it's important to continue reading. In most cases, you'll realize that our definition is different from what you might have thought.

Remember that our system requires different ways of thinking and working. So throughout Basic Training, I encourage you to put aside the definitions you already have for terms that we present and maintain an open mind. As a result, you'll gain the greatest benefit from what we offer you.

In summary, Basic Training will give you the tools and foundation to succeed in this business. It will give you key knowledge that will help get you started in our business and duplicate what you learn.

Chapter 5

The Home Visit

Our Homes Reveal Who We Are

Let's say that you enjoy spending time with a coworker. Tiffany is dedicated, very organized, and always professionally dressed, and she drives a beautiful car. Both of you decide to attend an office happy hour that brings your coworkers together. You offer to pick her up and carpool to the restaurant.

When you arrive at her house and enter it, it's one of the messiest places you've ever visited. Bills, old newspapers, and paperwork cover nearly every surface. Tiffany's clothes have been tossed all over the place, which makes it difficult to walk around.

You have difficulty matching your new impression of Tiffany with the one you had previously. "How can someone be so different at work and at home?" you wonder. Suddenly, your beliefs about her have changed.

If Tiffany were to join our business, we would ask that she and her business mentor complete a **Home Visit**. Here, the two would arrange to meet at Tiffany's house. This would help her business mentor have a better understanding of who she is, which is an important part of building skinship. In this chapter, you'll learn why Home Visits are a basic part of building Trust and Understanding. I'll also introduce you to the Personal Financial Checkup (PFC). You'll learn what it is and how it connects to the Home Visit.

What Is a Home Visit?

One of the basic steps to take before joining our business is to conduct a Home Visit. This involves your potential business mentor visiting you where you live and getting to know you and the people closest to you. The Home Visit is an important way for your business mentor to get to know the "real" you.

For most of us, our home tops our list of the most important places we spend our time. It's where we raise our kids, gather with family and friends, sleep, and return to after a long day's work. In this way, the home is often the dividing line between our private and public lives. Most organizations separate the two and believe that it's inappropriate to combine them. In fact, organizations commonly have the mindset that "what goes on at home is none of our business!" In other words, one's home life has no influence over one's work life.

But the Home Visit illustrates another way that we're different from the rest of the financial industry. We believe that your home life *does* influence your work life, and your work life influences your home life. If you hide this "other side" of your life from your business mentor, he or she will not be able to figure out what you truly need in order to succeed.

Meet the Most Important Person in Your Life

Building Trust and Understanding *isn't* like a coat that you take on and off. In fact, we think that Trust and Understanding are values that you maintain at work, at home, and wherever you go. Thus the Home Visit confirms your ability make Trust and Understanding a way of life for you. The main way it does this is through a step that we call **Meet the most important person in your life**. During this phase, your mentor will meet your spouse, significant other, or anyone else who will be affected by your commitment to our business. With the Home Visit, you and your mentor will make sure that this person approves of your decision.

For example, if you're committing fully to our business, the initial time investment will probably be significant, and sometimes your schedule won't fit within the 9-to-5 time frame. The last thing you want is to put in hours and hours building your team and your business, only to realize that your husband or wife doesn't support your involvement.

What if your spouse or significant other is angry rather than supportive of your time away? What if he or she doesn't believe that this is the right career for you? All these questions and more will influence your ability to succeed. You and your business mentor will use the Home Visit to determine whether or not you'll experience personal barriers in your business. Thus your business mentor's analysis will save you time and energy. He or she will help you figure out if your personal situation means that our business is not a good fit for you.

A Home Visit is also an opportunity to strengthen skinship. In the same way that an underwear story teaches others about you, your home tells a story as well. It reflects who you are and what's important to you. By visiting you at home, your mentor will learn your koraji.

In summary, the Home Visit allows your mentor to meet the most important person in your life, and it builds skinship. Together, these will prepare you and your mentor for the next step: the **Personal Financial Checkup** (PFC). The Home Visit is where you'll complete your PFC. As you'll discover in the next chapter, the PFC will be your guide as you and your mentor begin setting your professional goals.

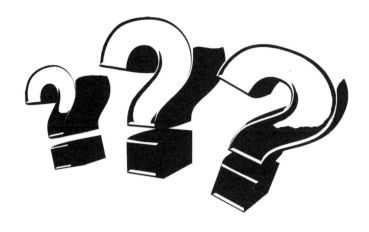

Chapter 6

The Personal Financial Checkup (PFC)

The **Personal Financial Checkup** is a basic list of questions that we use to examine a person's financial situation. The PFC is something that you'll complete with your business mentor, and it's one of the first steps to launching your business.

In the following section, you'll learn about the PFC and how it helps you set your professional goals. Then I'll explain how to use the PFC to help others.

Your PFC: You, Your Mentor, and the Home Visit

Using the PFC, you and your business mentor will figure out your income and expenses, what you own and what you owe, and more. It's part of the Home Visit process. This means that it may play a role in your first Home Visit or later ones—

this is for you and your mentor to decide. During the Home Visit, the PFC is focused on you. Later in your career, you will be conducting PFCs with those who may want to join your team or who may benefit from financial solutions you have to offer.

One of the main reasons that your PFC takes place during a Home Visit has to do with the comfort and peace of mind that our home gives us. Because the PFC addresses your personal finances, which are often a private matter, your home is where you'll most likely be open to sharing this information with your mentor.

Your PFC has the following three benefits:

1. It improves your financial koraji.
2. It speeds up your business goal setting.
3. It builds Trust and Understanding.

A PFC Improves Your Financial Koraji

"In the event that an oxygen mask appears in front of you, secure your mask first, and then help someone who requires assistance," the flight attendant announces. If you've ever taken a plane trip, you've heard a version of this message. Your PFC is like the oxygen mask that you place on yourself first. Once you're out of danger, you can then support those around you. But unless you're in good financial shape or you're working hard toward improving your financial state, you'll struggle to help others.

One of the most effective ways to improve others' lives is to "practice what you preach." In other words, if you're providing your clients the tools to upgrade their financial lives, it's important that your financial life is in solid shape. And remember that one day, you'll be a business mentor, too. Therefore, you want your professional and personal lives to be good examples to those you'll be guiding.

For instance, let's say that you hired a personal trainer who smoked cigarettes and was overweight. What if he or she insisted that you stop smoking and lose weight? You probably wouldn't follow the trainer's suggestions because an overweight personal trainer who smokes doesn't have a lot of credibility. But what if your personal trainer was in good shape and clearly followed his or her own advice? You would be more likely to listen to his or her recommendations. Similarly, you want your personal finances to reflect that your business can improve others' lives just as it has benefitted yours.

A PFC Is a Reality Check

Often, people don't realize how they're spending their money. They may have high credit card balances that they carry from month to month, and they can't explain why they have so much debt. If you asked what their financial goals were for the next one, five, and ten years, they wouldn't have a clue. But if you asked them something like, "Overall, what do you think about your finances right now?" they would answer, "I think everything's OK."

Your PFC, however, may show that everything *is not* OK. By going through the checklist, people often see that they need to make better financial decisions. And once they recognize the consequences of inaction—more debt, no retirement savings, no funds to cover an emergency, bankruptcy, and more—they're motivated to make changes and take action quickly.

A PFC Helps You Set Achievable Goals

As you've already learned, koraji is one of the first ingredients to building Trust and Understanding. Just as you need to know your koraji to develop lasting business relationships, you need to know financial koraji to set your achievable financial and business goals. And your PFC is the most important step to learning your financial koraji. Once you complete your PFC, you'll be able to figure out how fast you'll need to grow and the level of commitment you'll need in order to meet your financial goals. By doing so, you'll also learn how to help others accomplish their goals later on when you conduct PFCs for other people.

Completing your PFC is just as important to your business mentor as it is to you because your mentor will need to figure out how much training and help you need in order to get started. Your business mentor will combine his or her goal-setting experience with the information you provide. Based on the outcome of your checkup, your goals can vary widely. For instance, if you have three kids and a stay-at-home spouse, and your full-time job supports your entire family, your business mentor won't set goals that require you to commit 60 hours a week to our business. Instead, your business mentor will create a plan that takes into account that you already have a full-time job and a family. With proper goals in place, you'll be ready to improve your financial life.

I've seen the PFC turn around the lives of people who were in bad financial shape. Through working with a business mentor, they set realistic financial and career targets and worked tirelessly to accomplish them, and as a result, their lives have improved dramatically. A business mentor gave them a way to see how their past decisions had led to poor decision making. They used this information to change their habits. One of the most powerful outcomes of their experiences was that they were able to relate to others in a completely new way.

People like these have "been there, done that." In other words, when they meet people who need new solutions to financial problems, their example will help others see that our business can improve their lives.

In fact, going through a PFC often inspires people to want to reach out to their friends and family as soon as possible. They want to share what they've learned because they believe they can help those they care about. By completing their PFC with a business mentor, they're also learning how to use a PFC to help others. Thus mentorship prepares them to guide others faster than if they worked alone.

A PFC Requires Trust and Understanding

As you've learned, Trust and Understanding isn't just a slogan for us. This concept guides the way we operate, and it's probably one of the main factors that interested you in our business. In order for you to succeed, your mentor needs to know your financial circumstances, which means that you and your mentor must be able to trust one another. Allow me to give you an example.

Imagine that you have a business partner, and the two of you decide to open a restaurant together. From the start, you and Sam agree to split all expenses equally. You've spent months planning and saving your money, you've found a location, and your rental agreement has been accepted. Your landlord then asks for the first and last months' rent, and you write a check for your half.

You remind Sam that he needs to write his check, too. "No problem, just give me a few days," he says. A week passes, and your landlord requests the rest of the rental deposit. You ask Sam for the money again. At this point, he admits that he lost his savings because of poor investment decisions and cannot afford to open a restaurant. You can't believe what he just told you. "Why didn't Sam let me know earlier?" you ask yourself. Now you're left with only 50 percent of a business ready to go.

Although you and Sam agreed to open a restaurant together, you didn't know each other's financial situations. If Sam had completed a PFC prior to signing the rental paperwork, you would have known right away that he was saying one thing (let's open a restaurant) and doing another (running out of money). In addition, you wouldn't have felt the shock and disappointment of finding out about Sam's poor financial health at the worst possible time.

This example points to how your goals need to align with your actions, and it usually takes someone to show you how. Your business mentor will probably spend many hours helping you build your business. In order to make the best use of your time together, both of you need to understand your financial status, and the PFC will be your guide. The more honest and up-front you are about the good and bad aspects of your finances, the more you'll benefit from your mentor's expertise.

Two Common PFC Questions

Q1: Isn't a PFC getting too personal?

Eventually, you'll be going through PFCs with people who will want to join your team. These individuals will trust you with their financial information. Right now, it's *your* turn to go through it. When you go through the process yourself, you're learning about your financial koraji, and you're using it to set professional goals. You're receiving hands-on experience with the PFC process, you're building skinship, and you're showing your commitment to following the principles of our system. All four of these points are important to establish your business. Therefore, *the one who benefits most from the PFC is you.*

Q2: What if my PFC reveals areas in which I've made poor financial choices? Will this mean that this business isn't for me?

The short answer is no. In fact, if you find yourself in bad financial shape, our business may help you upgrade your life. And by learning from past mistakes and overcoming obstacles, your success story will be a great example to motivate others to improve their lives as well.

Your ability to relate to others is an important way to build your business. When people see that you understand their circumstances and that your life is proof of the power of our business, they'll be open to hearing about the solutions you can offer them. The key here is that *you've improved your own life, or you're successfully working toward improving it.* In other words, you "practice what you preach." After all, if you're buried under debt and are doing nothing about it, you may be able to relate to others who are in the same situation as you, but they probably will not feel confident that you're the best person to help them.

PFCs for Your Potential Team Members or Clients

Eventually, you'll learn how to conduct PFCs for other people. As a result, you'll help your potential team members and clients in the same way that your mentor guided you when you completed your own PFC. When you begin completing PFCs with potential team members and clients, it's important to know that the PFC for new team members is *very different from* a PFC for clients.

Before I point out the main difference between the two, I'll first explain how they're the same. Both a PFC that you complete with new team members and one that you complete with clients are focused on figuring out the other person's financial situation.

But the primary difference between the two is that a PFC with a potential team member goes to a deeper level than one you complete with a prospective client. Recall the Green Button Checklist that you learned about in Chapter 3. I provided you with a set of questions that helped you figure out if this business was for you. In this case, the items from the Green Button Checklist are the kinds of questions that you will ask potential team members during their PFC. In other words, the PFC that you'll complete with potential team members moves beyond just gathering financial information. It requires you to ask questions that will determine whether your potential team member is ready to join your business. These questions wouldn't be necessary for your clients, who are just looking for financial solutions. In fact, if you were that intense with a client, you would probably scare him or her away.

I've kept my explanation of the PFC short because your business mentor will be the best resource to answer your questions about how to conduct a particular PFC. In fact, until you're licensed and trained, you'll count on your business mentor to oversee the entire process with your clients.

The Home Visit and PFC: Trust and Understanding at Work

When I speak with new team members about our business, they often express concerns about the Home Visit and the PFC. You, too, may be asking yourself questions such as, "Is this really worth all the effort?" and "Will the Home Visit and PFC really benefit me?" No doubt these two steps are unlike how most other organizations operate. But Trust and Understanding aren't ordinary business principles, either. That's why we had to develop specific steps to make sure you experience the greatest benefit from our training system. Be assured that our approach has been proven to work for people just like you. Once you've completed the Home Visit and PFC, you'll realize why it's so important, which will make it worth any discomfort and inconvenience.

We're serious about your success. That's why the Basic Training system is made up of proven strategies to help you establish goals and experience a fulfilling career. Building Trust and Understanding, along with mentorship, make up the foundation of Basic Training. And the Home Visit and the PFC highlight the importance of both. In the next chapter, you'll learn about a checklist designed to ensure that you and your mentor cover the most important aspects of your career in our business. We call it the **Associate Checklist**.

Chapter 7

The Associate Checklist

Throughout your business career, you'll be responsible for completing checklists. You've learned about one checklist so far. Earlier in this book, you completed the Green Button Checklist. In this chapter, I'll introduce you to one more checklist that is very important in our business. At this point, you may be wondering why checklists are so valuable. Allow me to explain.

From "What will I buy at the grocery store?" to "How can we safely send an astronaut to the moon?" checklists are used by both ordinary people and experts to help them remember key tasks. Research has shown that checklists help us keep track of easily overlooked things, and they also break down very complicated procedures into simple steps. That's why checklists are a part of many successful companies. In our organization, we are also strong believers in the power of checklists. As long as you remain in our business, checklists will be one of the main ways that you measure and track your progress.

In healthcare, doctors and hospital staff use checklists to make sure that patients undergo safe procedures. In fact, studies have shown that using checklists prior to surgeries has improved operating room safety. It's not that doctors forget how to perform medical procedures. But because they must remember so much and their jobs are so demanding, it's nearly impossible for them to keep track of everything without a list.

Similarly, you and your business mentor are responsible for serving your clients' and team members' needs. Although we've strived to make the principles of our business easy to remember and learn, there are certain things that you're bound to forget. That's the reason behind our checklist. Although it includes important items, our main emphasis is on tasks that are often overlooked or forgotten. These are tasks that team members often say they'll "take care of later" because they have more important things to do. Unfortunately, later never comes.

Checklists ensure that everyone within our business follows the same system, which has proven results. Checklists prevent team members from making mistakes that are easily avoidable and regularly ignored, and that have consequences that can be very serious. In addition, checklists help our organization to run efficiently. So like any business that cares about maintaining its solid reputation, we have multiple checklists that cover key aspects of Basic Training. One of the most important is the **Associate Checklist**.

What Is the Associate Checklist?

Through training thousands of people, we've developed a list of the key training topics, business-building steps, and to-dos that are important when starting in our business. These items all appear in the Associate Checklist. We created this checklist with two goals in mind:

1. It Speeds Up the Training Process

Basic Training improves upon what I realized was wrong with the rest of the financial industry. We want you to succeed as quickly as possible, so take the checklist seriously, and you'll avoid the errors we made learning by trial and error.

2. It Sets You Up for Success

In order to make Trust and Understanding the foundation of your business, you must learn more about how we run our business. The Associate Checklist ensures that your business mentor is effectively covering the topics that you need to address in order to launch your business.

Trust the Associate Checklist

Basic Training is rooted in Trust and Understanding, and the Associate Checklist makes sure that you learn all the basics you need to get started. This includes information you will learn in classroom settings, with your business mentor, and in the real world. The checklist shows our commitment to giving you the tools you need in order to reach your goals.

As you look through the items on the list, there may be terms and subjects that you don't recognize. Don't worry, we've taken care of this for you in two ways. First, you'll learn about more Basic Training concepts in future chapters in this book. Second, your business mentor's role is to answer any questions you have.

Throughout this book, we've discussed the role of koraji and the importance of not letting your ego get in the way of your professional success. This checklist is one way to test your commitment to that idea. When you follow every step in the checklist, you avoid making unnecessary mistakes, most of which will get in the way of your ability to succeed. And when you feel tempted to skip steps, it's usually a result of your past experience or bad habits encouraging you to ignore the system. No matter what, I urge you to address every item despite the temptation to skip some. In the next chapter, you'll learn about the next Basic Training step, which is how to use your mentor's expertise to support your business.

Chapter 8

The Leverage Exchange

As you progress through Basic Training, you and your business mentor will develop skinship—and skinship is what creates Trust and Understanding. Your business mentor is committed to your success, and the steps you've taken so far have ensured that both of you are working hard to grow your team and build your client base.

Now you're ready to learn about one of our key marketing principles. In this chapter, I'll define the most important aspects of our approach, explain how they're different from most other business models in our industry, and describe how they can lead to long-term success.

A Short Overview of Prospecting

In order to best understand the strategies that I'll describe, you'll need a general background in how prospecting works.

Let's first begin with a definition. For most businesses, **prospecting** *is reaching out to people in order to grow a client base, a team, or both.* In order to prospect successfully, you have to figure out how to get in touch with others. There are two ways that most companies do this:

1. The cold marketing approach
2. The warm marketing approach

Cold marketing means that a business and its team reaches out to people they don't know. Cold marketing counts on contacting as many people as possible. As a result, this approach often uses commercials, online and print advertising, and cold-calling. Because this approach is impersonal, I believe that cold marketing teaches professionals to be impersonal and not care enough about each client.

Warm marketing means that an organization and its team reaches out to people they have some kind of connection with already. Those people may be friends, family, and colleagues. Rather than advertise, warm marketing focuses on networking with others and reaching out to people we already know.

Most of the financial services industry uses cold marketing. But we believe that warm marketing is the better way because it allows us to take advantage of the built-in Trust and Understanding between us and the people we contact. When there is Trust and Understanding, business gets started faster and flows more smoothly, and professionals care more about their clients. This is what separates our organization from others.

But warm marketing also has some flaws. For instance, your prospect may trust you because you've known each other for many years and maybe even for your entire lives. Although your prospect knows that you have his or her best interests at heart, the bottom line is that you're new to the financial industry. As a result, your prospect may not believe that you're the best person to serve his or her needs. One way to address this problem is through the "Wait and Learn" approach.

What Is "Wait and Learn"?

Throughout our country, thousands of people start off in other companies by sitting in windowless classrooms. The last thing these other major financial companies want is for these new people to mess up appointments by saying the wrong thing to potential clients. So they send them to intense training, where they spend weeks learning about financial products before they are allowed to talk to anyone. Meanwhile, they aren't making any money. Even if they're eager to reach out to prospects, they're told that they have to wait and learn more.

The benefit of "Wait and Learn" is that new people are well trained and have a consistent learning experience. The major downside is that after training, they may have plenty of classroom knowledge, *but they haven't learned how to apply it to the real world.*

As you know, it's one thing to watch a video on, say, how to snowboard. It's completely different to hop on one yourself and go downhill. I believe this is one of the worst things that can happen to a person who is new to our industry because it is very hard to succeed without real-world experience. That is why, in our business, we found a way to combine the benefits of Wait and Learn with hands-on experience. It's through what we call the **leverage exchange**, which, as the name indicates, is rooted in **leverage**. Leverage is what makes the leverage exchange work.

What Is Leverage?

The root of the word *leverage* is *lever*. A lever is what helps you lift things that you could not otherwise raise on your own. When others are helping you, they're like your lever. When you help others—for instance, through mentorship—you're their lever. Thus *leverage* means using another person. It also means benefitting from someone else's skill or ability. In our business, you're constantly switching between helping others and being helped. By leveraging others, you'll save time and increase your ability to turn prospects into clients and team members.

Leverage Requires Trust and Understanding

If you recall, the recipe for Trust and Understanding has four ingredients:

1. Koraji
2. Ssagaji
3. Skinship
4. Underwear Stories

Because of koraji, you know both your and your mentor's strengths and weaknesses. You know who can best handle a certain situation, and you trust that both of you are truly trying to help one another. With Trust and Understanding in place, you are ready to experience the benefits of the **leverage exchange**.

What Is the Leverage Exchange?

It took me over a decade in the financial industry to realize that I was missing a key part of success. I had spent years working hard and following the traditional model of doing business: I spent countless hours earning professional certificates, studying products, and learning sales skills. Although all this knowledge was important to my future success, I eventually reached a point at which my business couldn't grow very fast based on what I could do by myself.

In fact, I was working hard, but there was only so much that I could accomplish in a day. Teamwork changed this. Once I learned to build a team, my ability to grow seemed nearly limitless. This is an example of **scalability**. It's how one coffeehouse can become an international chain that is on nearly every corner of every large U.S. city. When you have a strong team, your ability to grow is far greater than what you could do on your own. And the leverage exchange is the secret to building a long-lasting and effective team.

No matter how much you learn in a classroom, in order to succeed you have to reach out to people so your team grows. You and your business mentor can work together using each other's strengths. When you're first beginning, the roles of you and your mentor are as follows:

You: You have a list of contacts that includes friends, family, colleagues, and others. When you contact these individuals, you will arrange a meeting that includes your mentor because he or she will provide valuable field training and help you have successful appointments and expand your team. You trust your business mentor with your contact list because you realize that the fastest way he or she can teach you how to succeed is to show you by example.

Your mentor: Your business mentor will invest time to teach you the principles of our business. He or she will be your guide. Your business mentor will attend the meetings you arrange with your contacts so that you can see how our business works. I've met business mentors who make huge sacrifices for their trainees. They give up their workdays in order to attend meeting with prospects who live hours away, and many of those meetings don't result in new clients or team members. In addition, by helping you, they may be missing out on opportunities to build their own teams.

This sharing of each other's strengths—between you and your mentor—is an example of the power of the leverage exchange. Using the leverage exchange will allow you to accomplish your goals faster than would otherwise be possible.

In my experience, even those with financial services backgrounds still benefit from the leverage exchange. This is because the Trust and Understanding approach requires a completely different way of working. Without a business mentor's support, you won't develop the habits and mindset that can become the foundation of success in your career. The leverage exchange shows how two people are using their strengths to help each other. Another way to describe this is by saying that they *leverage one another.*

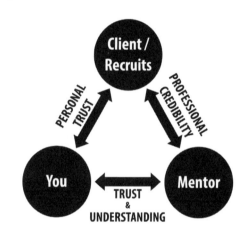

"The Perfect Environment"

A Plumber Starts in the Financial Industry

The following is an example of how the leverage exchange works.

Before beginning in our business, Steve had been a plumber for 20 years, which meant that he had a large network of contacts and customers. He was eager to launch his new career by growing his team and building a client base.

On one hand, Steve knew lots of people. On the other, if Steve reached out to his contacts right away, most would probably not feel confident that Steve could serve their financial needs. After all, to them he's "Steve the nice-guy plumber," not "Steve the financial expert." Here's a breakdown of Steve's strengths and weaknesses:

Strengths: Steve had a large network of contacts who had known him for years. Therefore, they trusted him.

Weaknesses: Steve was known as a plumber, not an expert in meeting the financial needs of his contacts. Therefore, his contacts did not want to talk to him about their finances.

Here's how the leverage exchange solved Steve's problems. Steve's mentor was Lisa. She had years of product knowledge and sales skills. Steve asked Lisa to help him set up the appointments and conduct presentations. Steve was able to overcome the doubts that his contacts had (this was his weakness) by telling them about Lisa's expertise and professional reputation (these were her strengths). As a result, Steve was able to address their doubts and set appointments. By leveraging Lisa's strengths, Steve was able to have successful appointments, build his team, and quickly learn the most important skills.

The Leverage Exchange Leads to Independence

Imagine that you owned the world's finest car, but because you couldn't drive it skillfully, you ended up getting into an accident. As far as your business is concerned, the leverage exchange helps you avoid career collisions. Using the car example, your mentor will teach you how to handle your car. He or she will then give you the keys when you're an expert driver yourself. As a result, you'll take control of your car and drive it like a pro.

The goal for both Steve and Lisa is that Steve will be able to eventually build his own team. By learning and observing Lisa and how she handles his contacts, he receives hands-on training. When he's ready, he'll be able to repeat the system that made Lisa a success. And at one point, he'll pass on his knowledge to future team members.

Now that you understand the leverage exchange and how it can benefit you as you start your career, I'll show you in the next chapter how to apply it to develop a prospecting list and plan appointments.

Chapter 9

Warm Market Prospecting

In our business, building relationships is our number one priority. This explains why Trust and Understanding are essential to how our clients and team members meet their personal and professional goals.

In the previous chapter, I defined prospecting as reaching out to people in order to grow a client base, a team, or both. The two ways that companies prospect are through **cold marketing** and **warm marketing**. Cold marketing emphasizes contacting as many people as possible, most of whom learn about the business through advertising and cold-calling. Before the first point of contact—whether through an online or print ad, TV commercial, or sales call—most prospects know little, if anything at all, about the organization.

Warm marketing is different, and I believe it is more effective. It's about building on relationships that already exist. In our business, we take warm marketing a step further. Our team members reach out not just to their professional contacts but to their friends and family, too. Warm marketing is the core business-building strategy for our team members, and we're passionate about it. In fact, because we don't focus on expensive advertising campaigns, the success of our organization depends on the relationships we create and maintain.

Why Our Prospecting System Is So Effective

Our warm marketing method has improved the lives of team members and their clients. Part of what makes it so easy to implement is its simplicity. The following are the features of our prospecting system:

1. It builds on leverage.
2. It's based on your koraji.
3. It's quickly learned and repeated, which leads to independent team members.

It Builds on Leverage

Leverage means you're using your own skills and abilities or those of someone else to your greatest advantage. With leverage, you alternate between helping others and being helped.

You help your business mentor by providing him or her with a wide network of people you know. Your mentor helps you by providing his or her expertise, which will help you grow your team or client base. He or she is also teaching you the most important parts of our business.

In addition, because you're new to our business, you still need to establish your experience and expertise. Fortunately, your mentor has "been there, done that." In other words, your mentor has learned our prospecting system from the first step (building a list) to the last step (using it to build a great team). He or she will be by your side to answer questions and teach you essential skills.

It's Based on Your Koraji

Your business mentor knows your koraji, which includes your career goals. Koraji is important because both you and your mentor need to understand what you want to accomplish in order to develop your prospecting plan.

For example, your needs will vary based on whether this is a **dual career** or a **full-time** endeavor. *Dual career* means that a large part of your work time is committed to another activity. For instance, you may be a substitute teacher in the public education system, which consumes 18 hours of your week, or you may be a parent of an infant or toddler. Meanwhile, *full time* means that this business is your top work priority, and you have at least full-time hours to devote to it.

It's Quickly Learned and Repeated, Which Leads to Independent Team Members

We believe that our warm marketing approach is far more effective and faster to learn than typical cold marketing methods. Cold marketing counts on you and you alone. In this case, the amount you can grow is limited by how much you can invest in advertising, which is typically expensive, especially at the beginning. In addition, without mentorship, you're responsible for expanding your team by yourself.

In contrast, our warm marketing system is made up of proven, simple strategies to build your team. By following our approach, your ability to grow isn't limited to how much money you can spend on advertising. In fact, you don't have to invest a penny on it. Thus you're only limited by how much time and energy you can commit to building your team and client base. In addition, working with your mentor will speed up the training process so that you'll experience results faster than you would by working alone. Our system also helps you avoid mistakes that could get in the way of your ability to reach your goals.

Lastly, because our system is made up of basic steps, it's simple to duplicate and teach to new team members. Eventually, you'll be able to expand your team independently.

Your Role in the Prospecting Process

The relationships you've developed over your lifetime are as individual as your fingerprints. Thus your prospects are yours and yours only. With that said, it takes a business mentor to help you develop your **prospecting list**. Your prospecting list is made up of people you'll contact—either to become team members or clients. It's what turns *the idea* of building your team and gaining clients into a *real task* that can be tracked and measured.

Keep in mind that *the most important reason you and your business mentor will invest time in your prospecting list is to set up* ***appointments***. An appointment is a meeting that you arrange with your contacts in order to present them with financial solutions or career opportunities. These meetings will be between your prospect, your business mentor, and you.

When you're starting out, remain open-minded and follow your business mentor's suggestions. Allow your business mentor to teach you the process. Once you've become a master prospector, you'll be able to take complete charge of creating your prospecting lists. This won't happen right away; it will take hard work and the guidance of your business mentor.

Your Business Mentor's Role in the Prospecting Process

Your business mentor will not only be your guide as you develop your prospecting list, but he or she will also be there during your first few appointments. Your business mentor has two main responsibilities. He or she:

1. Gives you greater opportunities to expand your team or your client base.
2. Teaches you how to eventually expand your team and client base on your own.

You may have the greatest prospecting list on the planet, but unless you're able to effectively provide your prospects with a reason to join your team or become a client, your list will be useless.

The prospecting system is what will keep your business growing, and it will also help create long-term success. The next step is to take the system and apply it to developing a prospecting list. In the next chapter, you'll learn how to do this.

Trust and Understanding: The Foundation of Our Prospecting Success

Our prospecting system takes the best of the approaches that are already out there and makes those methods even more effective. Therefore, I encourage you to read the next chapter carefully, write down questions you have, and share them with your business mentor. Put all these principles into practice and *resist the temptation to "reinvent the wheel."* When you have doubts about the system, discuss these with your business mentor so he or she can provide the insights you're looking for.

Prospecting Principles

Are you willing to do what it takes to succeed in the Leadership Game?

Goal Setting

Ssagaji

Are you aligned with your leaders?

What are your duties as a leader?

Discipline

What are your goals versus your team members' goals?

Are you challenging yourself every day?

Who is your business mentor?

Is your business moving every day?

Alignment results from accountability

Koraji

Do not reinvent the wheel

Walk the Walk, Talk the Talk, & Act the Act

Layers of mentorship

Building takes years of mastering

Skinship with leadership

Mentorship

Chapter 10

Prospect List and Hot Buttons

"John, I don't know anyone," new team members will often complain when I ask them whom they plan to reach out to. No doubt, it can seem like a huge challenge to develop a list. In order to create as many opportunities as possible for you, we've developed a system that will help you create better results. In this chapter, you'll learn about the **Top 25** and **Top 5** lists. The goal of both is to provide you with a group of contacts who will become either your clients or team members. Your business mentor will be your guide throughout the process. Once you master the process of creating Top 25 and Top 5 lists, you'll count on those skills over and over to grow your business throughout your entire career.

Two Types of Prospects

The following are the main groups of people we contact:

Potential clients: These people are possibly interested in the products and services we offer.

Potential team members: These people are interested in joining our business.

Although the needs of these two groups may be different, *how* you develop your prospecting list for both is the same: You begin by *thinking of as many people you know as possible.*

How Many People Do You Know?

Rather than worry about who you *don't know,* you and your business mentor will focus on who you *do know.* We developed a way to help with this. It starts with a simple question:

How many people do you know?

Many of you will answer "not many," while some of you will have a few people in mind. In either case, the Memory Jogger on the next page will get you thinking about your possibilities.

For example, if you thought you only knew 10 people, the Memory Jogger might add 10 more to your list. If you didn't think you knew anyone, going through the Memory Jogger will create a pleasantly surprising result.

MEMORY JOGGER

FAMILY & FRIENDS...
1. aunts and uncles
2. best friend
3. best friend's parents
4. siblings
5. in-laws
6. cousins
7. grandparents
8. siblings' in-laws

WHO...
1. was in your fraternity or sorority?
2. is very ambitious?
3. is the life of the party?
4. is known by everyone in town?
5. was in your wedding party?
6. has a high-profile job?
7. are your college friends?
8. has been laid off?
9. hates to lose?

THINK OF PEOPLE WHO OWN OR RUN...
1. dry cleaners
2. hotels
3. restaurants
4. convenience stores
5. gas stations
6. tanning salons

THINK OF PEOPLE YOU KNOW AT...
1. church
2. the gym
3. prior jobs
4. volunteer groups

THINK OF PEOPLE WHO SOLD YOU YOUR...
1. car
2. Internet service
3. mobile phone
4. software
5. car insurance
6. furniture
7. boat

THINK OF PEOPLE YOU KNOW, SUCH AS...
1. accountants
2. doctors
3. electricians
4. cab drivers
5. landlords
6. massage therapists
7. graphic artists
8. nurses
9. mail carriers
10. bartenders
11. locksmiths
12. homebuilders
13. firefighters

What to Consider as You Develop Your Top 25

Your business mentor will be your guide as you develop your Top 25 list. He or she will help you take your broader list and separate your stronger prospects from weaker ones. This process is very important, and both of you will invest time putting this list together. Think of it as yet another opportunity to build skinship. With your business mentor's help, you may realize that some of your "hot prospects" weren't as "hot" as you thought. Meanwhile, you may see that some of your weak prospects are actually worth pursuing.

Also, as you go through your list for the first time, it's important to save the names that you may have decided weren't part of your initial Top 25. That way, you can refer to them later when you put together more prospect lists in the future. After all, the future is unpredictable. You may become closer to people you had previously crossed off your list, they may turn out to be powerful referral sources, or both (you'll learn about referrals in Chapter 14).

1. Focus on Your Natural Market

As you've already learned, our business is rooted in Trust and Understanding. Our prospecting system is as well. Thus an important question to ask yourself when you're starting the prospecting process is, "Who in my life have I built Trust and Understanding with already?" The answer to this question is your **natural market**. The word *natural* commonly describes how something doesn't take much work to develop. For example, when something comes naturally to you, it doesn't require you to think much about it. You may be naturally good at meeting new people. Or you may be naturally skilled at remembering the names of people you've just met. Your natural market should come just as easily to you.

A powerful advantage of your natural market is that because it's made up of people you trust and understand, you already know how our business can help them.

2. Expand Your List Beyond Friends and Family

The people closest to you, such as your friends and family, will probably make it to the top of your natural market list. But with every rule comes an exception to it. Accept the fact that a strong prospect list may include more than just your natural market. In fact, as your career progresses and as you get to know more and more people, you may find that those who previously weren't part of your natural market suddenly make it onto your list. As I stated earlier, the future is unpredictable. Friends get married, people have kids, couples get divorced—our lives and our needs continually change. So maintain an open mind.

3. "Six Degrees of Separation"

This concept describes how we are all no more than six people (degrees) away (separated) from knowing anyone. Even if that person is on the other side of the planet, you're somehow connected to him or her through your relationship with someone else.

New team members often think of someone who could make their Top 25 list and then say, "But that person won't care about what I have to share." I've made this mistake, too. But people are more open-minded than you think. In fact, what might be missing in your relationship with that person is Trust and Understanding. Once you've established it, you may be able to turn a prospect into a team member. In addition, a prospect may not express interest, but you may discover that he or she knows someone who will. The lesson is to think of as many people as you can and try to find a connection to those people.

4. Look for a High Center of Influence

The **center of influence** principle shows how six degrees of separation is important. While the person you're contacting may not be interested in what our business has to offer, he or she may know someone who is. When people have a high center of influence, it means they are respected by and know many other people. For example, if you know a local business owner, she probably has a network of people who trust and respect her. Or if you know the head of a volunteer organization, he most likely has solid ties within the community. These types of individuals are great to have on your list because even if they do not need your help, they probably know people who do.

5. Get Rid of the "Lottery Mindset"

You might be positive that one person on your list will make you rich. This is what we call a "lottery mindset." Mr. or

Ms. Prospect has a high center of influence and is very hard-working. In my experience, however, no one prospect has ever made a team member rich. Your prospect may be the first one to do this, but the chances are very slim. The danger of the lottery mindset is that you might put all your energy into one person. And when that prospect doesn't turn out to be as amazing as you expected, you'll be left very disappointed and also with no new business. The way to avoid this is to focus your attention on your entire prospecting list rather than any particular individual on it. In other words, the list is more important than any one person.

6. Imagine Teaching, Not Selling

When most new team members think of whom they should contact first, they usually imagine people who have a high likelihood of listening to their sales pitch. This, however, can make you rule out certain people who may actually be very interested in what you have to say. The best advice I ever received about prospecting was to think about who would be interested in what I had to say, even if they never bought anything from me. So rather than think, "I can sell to (insert name here)," ask yourself, "Who do I know who is open to learning new information from my business mentor and me?" Quite often, you will discover that people don't really know what they want or need until you talk to them and ask them questions.

7. Prospecting Is a Permanent Process

Throughout your career, you will always create new prospecting lists. Thus once you've mastered the Top 25 process, you'll repeat it over and over again as you meet new people, and you'll revise your list as people you know undergo changes in their lives. Therefore, learning to create a Top 25 list is central to your prospecting system as well as to the future success of your business.

From 25 to 5: Your Top 5 List Builds Confidence

You and your business mentor will now determine whom, out of your Top 25 people, you'll approach first. This list is typically 5 people, and they are the ones who are most likely to either join your team or become a client. The Top 5 list helps you build your team and client base quickly. Think of it as your start-up list. These are the people who will help you build your confidence as you apply our prospecting system to the real world.

To provide a personal finance comparison, think of the Top 5 as you would a debt-cutting plan. One way to tackle paying down your debt is to get rid of the biggest loan first. From there, you would pay off the smaller ones. While this approach has its strengths, it can also be very time consuming and provide little immediate gratification. In fact, it may be months, or even years, before you pay off the biggest debt.

But you could approach it in the opposite way: Pay off the smaller debts first. This way, you'll see the immediate results of your work and have the confidence to continue. The Top 5 list is similar to this approach. It gives you a chance to learn about our business quickly and experience success as you learn our prospecting system. Inevitably, once you meet with 5 people, you'll create additional opportunities to meet with even more prospects. The doors you can open are endless.

The following is one of the exercises that will help you determine your Top 5:

Imagine that your house was burning down and it was filled with your closest friends and family. If you could only rescue your family and one other person, who would that one other person be?

Sometimes extreme examples are the best way to make a point. That "one other person" would probably land a spot on your Top 5 list. But your Top 5 list can also include people you've built Trust and Understanding with who are outside your circle of close friends and family.

For example, suppose that you knew your mail carrier. In the past when you chatted with Rita as she delivered your mail, she shared that she was worried that she wouldn't have enough savings to retire comfortably. Now you can say something like, "Hey, Rita, I know someone who may be able to provide a solution for you." That "someone" is your business mentor. Rita is interested in learning more, and as a result, you arrange a meeting between Rita, your business mentor, and you.

A Top 5 list makes it easier to get comfortable with prospecting. You may be very motivated when you first launch your business, but setting up appointments isn't easy, and you may find yourself reluctant to start prospecting. But if you experience early successes, you'll feel inspired to keep moving forward.

Shouldn't I Save My Best Prospects for Myself?

Let's say that one of your prospects seems to have an expensive lifestyle. You know that he lives in a nice neighborhood and owns a big house. From what you can tell, this prospect is a "sure thing." You also recognize that you don't have enough experience or professional credibility to successfully turn him into a client. At the same time, you're reluctant to share this contact with your business mentor. After all, why share something when you can have it all to yourself?

In this case, I believe that leverage still works. (If you recall, leverage means that you're using your own skill or ability or that of someone else to your greatest advantage.) First of all, your business mentor's extensive experience provides you with the best chance of closing the sale or expanding your team. Without him or her, you may not know how to answer your prospect's questions.

Meanwhile, your business mentor is sacrificing his or her time to attend a meeting with an uncertain outcome. For instance, I've attended countless "sure thing" appointments with people I'm mentoring. They insist that the prospect will definitely join our team or become a client. During the meeting, I've asked a few careful questions based on my years of speaking with countless prospects. As a result, I quickly figured out that the prospect was supporting his or her lifestyle with credit cards and debt. The "sure thing" ended up being a waste of time.

But if you're still not convinced...

A basic part of Trust and Understanding is recognizing that your business mentor is looking after your best interests. Thus providing your list will reap *long-term rewards* because doing so will help you learn how to build your business quickly. Furthermore, you can only go so far with your prospecting list when you are brand new and don't have much credibility to convince people to join your team or become your client.

In my experience, people with no financial background might be lucky to get one or two sales or recruits on their own after going through their entire Top 25. But even the most stubborn people usually realize that using your whole list for one or two people isn't the best or even the fastest way to start a long-term career. With your business mentor's support, however, you'll accomplish much more than you can on your own because you'll be working with someone who can show you how to build the business properly and use the entire list properly.

Your business mentor is taking time to teach you how to build a business, and you're gaining the skills that will lead to your long-term success. In exchange, you're giving your business mentor opportunities to grow his or her team. Meanwhile, your business mentor may be missing out on opportunities to grow his or her team because he or she is investing time to support you. When you understand this exchange, the tradeoff of providing your list is small compared to the benefits you'll experience for the life of your career.

Despite this, some people may still wonder, "Why should I share my list when it just means that my business mentor might be making money off me!" Saying or feeling something like this usually shows that the new team member isn't confident about our prospecting approach. If you have doubts like these, the best solution is for you to do what feels most comfortable. The bottom line is that you're establishing a new career, and you want to feel confident about the professional choices you're making.

Furthermore, when new team members express concerns about this part of the prospecting process, it usually indicates a lack of Trust and Understanding between the new team member and his or her business mentor. In most instances, when a business mentor hasn't properly built Trust and Understanding or tries to push someone before he or she is ready, the new team member usually *has doubts* about our business system.

Thus your willingness to follow the prospecting system shows whether your business mentor followed the Trust and Understanding process correctly. If you're unsure about it, your business mentor most likely needs to go back and make sure he or she built enough Trust and Understanding about our prospecting system before moving forward.

I've Developed My List...Now What?

As I shared earlier, *the most important reason that you and your business mentor will invest time into your prospecting list is to set up appointments.* Planning ahead is the most effective way to create appointments that will provide the best possible results. Successful planning requires open and frequent communication between you and your business mentor. When you're first starting in our business, your business mentor will be your source for guidance and information. This is another example of leverage. You are sharing your prospect list with your business mentor, and he or she is teaching you the most important parts of our business. You and your business mentor will work together to develop a prospecting plan.

An essential step in developing a prospecting plan is to figure out your prospect's **hot buttons**. Hot buttons are the specific concerns and needs of your prospect. Hot buttons include topics related to the prospect's age, goals, personal circumstances, and more. For example, does the prospect have a spouse and kids? What type of career experience does he or she have?

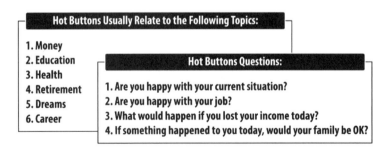

Hot Buttons Usually Relate to the Following Topics:
1. Money
2. Education
3. Health
4. Retirement
5. Dreams
6. Career

Hot Buttons Questions:
1. Are you happy with your current situation?
2. Are you happy with your job?
3. What would happen if you lost your income today?
4. If something happened to you today, would your family be OK?

Invest time in figuring out your prospect's hot buttons. Here, you can count on your business mentor's experience and help. He or she will help you determine what your prospect's hot buttons are. Hot buttons are one of the keys to having successful appointments. Your business mentor will use the information you've gathered to determine the best way to approach your prospect. Through figuring out your prospect's hot buttons, your business mentor will also know what questions and concerns to expect during an appointment.

In terms of the prospects who form your natural market, you probably know their hot buttons already. Earlier I provided the example of Rita, your mail carrier. If your business mentor were to ask, "What's Rita's hot button?" you'd immediately be able to say, "She's worried about her retirement." Or if your sister-in-law were on your prospect list, you might already know that she was looking for a way to earn money that would allow her to maintain the responsibilities that come with being a mom of two young children.

But there might be people on your prospect list whose hot buttons you don't know yet. It'll take work to figure them out, but it's essential to do this. Your business mentor will then help you develop a plan to contact them and learn more about them.

From Hot Buttons to Setting Up Appointments

So far you and your business mentor have worked hard to develop your prospect list. You've identified your prospects' hot buttons and have shared them with your business mentor. Now all your preparation will be put to good use. It's time to reach out to your prospects.

At this point, you're probably very excited to share about how our business has helped you and how you believe it will help your prospects. You may not be certain whether your prospects will be potential team members or clients. In fact, they may be neither, but they might know someone who would be interested. In the next chapter, you'll learn how to use your prospecting list to grow your client base and team.

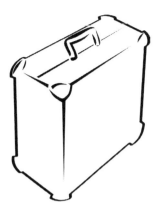

Chapter 11

Appointments

You've been there countless times. Sitting. Waiting. Eager to get all your questions answered. Anticipating that your name will be called next. Overall, you're grateful to be there. In fact, you scheduled your entire day around arriving on time to your doctor's appointment.

Now imagine the following scenario: Your doctor arrives at your house. He stands patiently at your front door, hoping that you'll open the door and meet him at the time you told him you were available.

"That wouldn't happen in a million years!" you insist. And you're probably right. But this is the strange prospecting approach that millions of people have been taught: Knock on doors, cold-call, wait, and repeat until someone shows interest. Wouldn't it be nice to have your prospects *wanting* to meet you because they're interested in what you have to share? In this chapter, you'll learn how to reap the rewards of conducting business (and prospecting) based on Trust and Understanding. The work you've done so far will create countless opportunities for you to grow your business.

A Review of the Prospecting Process

If you recall, prospecting is reaching out to people in order to grow a client base, a team, or both. So far, you've worked with your business mentor to develop a prospecting list, and you've identified your prospects' hot buttons.

How you'll move through the next steps of the prospecting process depends on which of the following three categories your prospects will fit under:

1. Potential team members
2. Potential clients
3. "I'm not sure which"

So how do you know whether your prospect is a potential team member or client? Your business mentor will be your guide. Through working with your business mentor, you'll learn how to use your prospects' **hot buttons** to determine which category suits them best.

For review, hot buttons are the special concerns and needs of your prospects. You can identify hot buttons because you've invested in skinship. The more skinship you've developed with your prospects, the easier it is to know their hot buttons and reach out to them.

For instance, if your prospect wants to improve his or her financial situation, that's a clue that he or she might be interested in joining your team. But if your prospect is more interested in how he or she can use financial products or services, your prospect will most likely fit in the client category.

With that said, you and your business mentor may not always know whether your prospect will fit into category one or two. Or, based on his or her hot buttons, your prospect may even fit into both. In addition, your prospect may not be sure which path would be best for him or her. One of the goals of the **appointment** may be to figure out the most appropriate category your prospect will fit in and to align the solutions you provide to meet his or her needs.

What Is an Appointment?

An appointment is a meeting that you arrange with a prospect in order to give him or her information about financial solutions or career opportunities. You schedule this meeting ahead of time with someone from your prospecting list.

Appointment and Prospecting Process

The two charts are general guides to help you understand the process for a potential team member or client. Although each item appears once, you may need to repeat one or more of them many times in order to build a long-term connection with a particular prospect. For instance, increasing skinship may require you to do a few Drop-bys, appointments, or both.

At the beginning of your career, you'll most likely find yourself wanting to follow the steps in the order they appear. As you gain experience, however, you'll discover times when you'll go through the steps in a different order, or you'll skip some steps altogether.

Regardless of your approach, it's the end result that counts. If your prospect has joined your team or has become your client, your method was effective. In this sense, prospecting is more art than science. In other words, there are certain rules to stick to, such as setting up appointments, but your prospect's particular needs will influence how you move through the process. It's up to you and your business mentor to develop a path that will create the best possible outcome.

Next, I'll describe the following new terms that appear in the two charts: **Drop-by** and **BPM**.

What Is a Drop-By?

Think of this as a "casual appointment" in which parts of the meeting can change and there is no expectation of immediate results. The role of a Drop-by is to give you a chance to get to know a prospect in the event that he or she might not be ready for a "real" appointment or meeting with a formal presentation.

In other words, this is how you develop skinship and learn more about the person. The Drop-by might also give you a chance to introduce your business mentor to your prospect in a casual way. The location of a Drop-by may be anywhere from a local coffeehouse to a conference room or even a prospect's home.

There are two reasons we use the Drop-by. First, new team members who have little appointment-setting experience may be reluctant and nervous to arrange a "real" appointment with a formal presentation and an expectation of immediate results. Thus, the Drop-by is a way to slowly develop confidence. Second, the Drop-by occurs when you don't know the prospect well. In this instance, the Drop-by is a form of **ice breaking**, which means that it helps you and your prospect get to know each other better.

Although we provide the Drop-by as a step, we don't think you'll need to use it often. If you continually reach out to prospects with high **centers of influence**, you will have a stream of solid prospects to add to your prospecting list. If you recall, when people have a high center of influence, it means they are respected and known by many people. You'll learn more about the role that these people play in your prospecting in Chapter 14: Referrals.

Common Ways to Drop By

You and your business mentor will determine which of the following approaches to take. You may do any combination of these steps:

1. Get to know the prospect and find out about his or her hot buttons.
2. Bring materials to discuss when you meet.
3. Talk about your business mentor and our business. If the prospect is interested, have your business mentor stop by, introduce him- or herself, and drop off material to your prospect.

What Types of Material Do I Use?

The purpose of the Drop-by is to establish skinship and create interest in what our business has to offer. Thus the materials you use should support your efforts. It always helps to know about your prospect's interests and needs. That way, you can drop off a certain brochure, book, video presentation, article, or other financial information that you believe will be helpful to your prospect. When you follow up with him or her, you can ask something like, "What did you think about what you read (or saw)?"

Always Leverage Your Business Mentor During Drop-Bys

Your business mentor's presence in the Drop-by is optional. If your business mentor will be a part of it, you'll first let him or her know about your plans. As a result, he or she will then be available to drop by and meet your prospect in the event that the opportunity arises. If your business mentor isn't part of the Drop-by, you'll regularly bring up your business mentor's expertise during your conversation with your prospect.

Whether or not your business mentor is there during your Drop-by, your goal isn't to close a deal. Instead, it's to build skinship and figure out hot buttons. Thus a successful Drop-by can mean that you'll arrange another Drop-by, a formal appointment that includes your business mentor, or an invitation to a **BPM**.

What Is a BPM?

The **Business Presentation Meeting** (BPM) is a weekly event where you, your team members, and invited guests gather. It's a consistent and powerful place to introduce your prospects to our business. The BPM was designed to move your prospects forward with regard to your prospecting plans. Thus it should play a central role in your business. In Chapter 12, I'll explain how to invite your prospects to a BPM and how you can use a BPM to set more appointments. For now, let me continue and explain the rest of the prospecting process.

Step by Step Toward Results

The Drop-by is the most informal step in the prospecting process. The less you know your prospects, the more you need to get to know them, and informal steps may be the best way to do this. But, if you've already built skinship with your prospects or you already know them very well, the informal steps may not be necessary.

For example, if you know very little about your prospects,

you'll probably not be able to successfully arrange an appointment right away. Your first step may be to drop off a book that your prospects may be interested in reading. Next, you may meet them for lunch, where your business mentor will join you. Afterward, you'll invite your prospects to a BPM. Then you'll arrange an appointment that includes you, your prospects, and your business mentor at a casual location, such as a local coffeehouse, or perhaps you'll schedule a Home Visit.

Always Generate Interest

Regardless of whether you are doing a Drop-by, appointment, BPM, or Home Visit, it is important to remember that one of your main goals is to generate interest from your prospect.

Imagine that you are a doctor. Kelly, your patient, has been diagnosed with skin cancer. Like most people, she is very worried. In this case, her hot button is "How will this disease affect me?" You've built skinship with her, so you know this. As a result, you ask, "Kelly, have you heard about this new skin cancer treatment?" Instantly, she's curious and asks, "No, can you tell me more?"

You don't have to convince her that you have information that may benefit her. You don't feel pressured to speak as fast as possible due to fear that she'll lose interest. In fact, you'll speak calmly and at a relaxed pace because Kelly is listening to your every word and can't wait to hear more.

You have Kelly's full attention because what you are saying

matches her hot-button topics. You have earned Kelly's trust, and she looks to you as a reliable person to help her. Doing the opposite—*not* matching your talk with her hot buttons—is sloppy and will damage your credibility. Using the cancer treatment example, a sloppy question would sound something like this: "Kelly, I'm not sure what kind of disease you have, but I know I can help you with anything." Now Kelly is doubtful that you understand her needs.

So how do you make sure that you've identified the right hot buttons and have used them correctly? You leverage your business mentor's expertise. He or she will use the information you've gathered about your prospect to create topics that will get your prospect interested in our business and what we have to offer. Once you've developed a plan with your business mentor, you're ready to reach out to your prospects. In the next section, I'll explain how to do this.

Invitation Principles: How Do I Invite Prospects to an Appointment?

Each connection you have with a prospect is different. Some prospects are your closest friends and family members, while others you may not know very well yet. Thus there's no "best way" to arrange an appointment. One thing, however, will always be the same: You'll always use your prospecting list as a guide.

If your prospect is someone you talk to regularly, the invitation may be as easy as sending a text message. But if your prospect is someone less familiar, you may need a more in-depth approach, such as a phone call or asking him or her in person. When you're uncertain about what method to follow, seek your business mentor's advice.

Here are some general guidelines regarding invitations:

1. Be Proud of What You Do!

Always remind yourself how fulfilling it is to be part of our business. Allow this feeling to inspire you to proudly reach out to your prospects and arrange appointments so they can learn more about how you can help them.

2. Focus Only on Setting Up the Appointment

Don't use your conversation as a way to figure out right away whether they'll join your team or become your client. As you build skinship, this information will come to you naturally.

3. Keep the Conversation Short

You should usually limit the conversation to five minutes. Any longer and you risk saying too much. Often what happens when the conversation runs too long is that you become focused on sharing everything you know about our business. This leads your prospect to ask questions, which pushes you to provide answers, which results in even more questions. In the end, you may end up providing incorrect information, or you may accidentally say something that discourages your prospect from agreeing to meet.

4. Appointment-Setting Secret: Create Curiosity

You may sometimes feel uncomfortable contacting your prospects to set up appointments. "Why would they want to talk to me?" you may ask yourself. Think of it this way: **First**, do a good job of using your hot buttons to guide you on what to say. **Next**, your prospects will become curious about our business without your having to say too much (see Principle 3). **Lastly**, you'll be pleasantly surprised that they'll *actually want* to meet with you. An effective way to create curiosity is to say enough about our business to interest them but not enough to answer all their questions. It's a delicate balance.

Throughout your short conversation, you want to speak highly of your business mentor whenever possible. Be sincere about what makes your business mentor a great resource for information, and don't be afraid to share about his or her other positive qualities. By doing so, you'll increase his or her credibility in the eyes of your prospect. For instance, if your prospect asks you something, you can respond with: "That's a great question. My business mentor can give you a far better answer than I can because he has years of experience dealing with those situations." That way, you're not only avoiding giving an inaccurate response, but you're also building up your business mentor's credibility and providing your prospect with a solution. It's as if you're saying, "Hey Prospect, if you agree to meet, I'll make sure we address your questions during our appointment."

Your Role and Your Business Mentor's Role

As far as the agenda items of the appointment are concerned, your business mentor will guide you through what needs to be covered during each appointment as well as how to do it. During the meeting, the responsibilities that each of you will have are as follows:

Responsibility	You	Mentor
Inspire prospects to learn more about our business.	√	√
Share about what it's like to be part of our business.	√	√
Teach basic financial concepts.		√
Watch and learn about the appointment process.	√	

Prior to the appointment, if you and your business mentor haven't figured out which category your prospect fits into (see "An Overview of the Prospecting Process" in this chapter), you'll use this meeting to find out. Thus this appointment may focus on asking questions and getting to know the prospect rather than closing the deal.

Appointment Dos and Don'ts

Working together with your business mentor on appointments is key to learning how to eventually run appointments independently (in other words, without your business mentor). During meetings with your prospects, you'll observe how your business mentor works. Learning from him or her will help you branch out on your own and teach others. In order to get the most out of your time with your business mentor, we've created a basic list of "dos and don'ts" to keep in mind:

Before the Appointment, Keep in Mind the Following:

1. Always take pride in our business and use it to inspire you to always do your best.
2. Prior to the appointment, let your prospect know that your business mentor will attend the meeting, too.
3. Speak highly of your business mentor whenever interacting with your prospect because this will help build his or her credibility.
4. Arrive 15 minutes before the appointment and make sure you and your business mentor arrive together so you both appear professional and prepared.

During Appointment, Do the Following:

1. Introduce your business mentor to your prospect right away.
2. Help your prospect connect with your business mentor by handling the introductions. For more on this topic, refer to "Icebreaking and Announcements" in Chapter 12.
3. If you're recruiting a new team member, make sure that "the most important person in your life" is there. For more information, refer to "Meet the Most Important Person in Your Life" in Chapter 5.
4. Leave it up to your business mentor to determine where everyone in the meeting will sit in order to create an effective meeting environment.

5. Allow your business mentor to spend at least 15 minutes getting to know your prospect.
6. If you're meeting at the prospect's home, figure out which area will make your appointment the most effective and politely recommend that you meet there. This is a place with as few distractions as possible and one that has a table and chairs. A dining room or kitchen is typically the best place.
7. If young children are disrupting the meeting, consider offering to take them aside and supervise them while your business mentor talks with your prospect.
8. Observe your business mentor carefully throughout the meeting. Remain quiet and take notes during the appointment.

During Appointments, *Avoid* the Following:

1. *Do not* interrupt the meeting or look unprofessional by asking questions of your own. Instead, write them down and discuss them with your business mentor afterward.
2. *Do not* run late. If being late is unavoidable, be sure to let your prospect know through a phone call or text message.
3. *Do not* dress too casual or sloppy. Aim for a professional look.
4. *Do not* wear strong cologne or perfume that may distract the prospect.
5. *Do not* chew gum.
6. *If possible, avoid using* the prospect's phone or bathroom.

7. *Do not* bring or use recording devices or cameras because it will make the prospect less likely to talk openly.

Appointments Are Usually Baby Steps Toward Your Destination

When you're meeting with your prospect, sometimes he or she will give you a clear-cut answer such as, "No, I'm not interested. Never contact me again," or "Yes! Sign me up right away!" In most instances, however, your prospect will fall somewhere in between those two extremes. It's important to maintain *balance* and *flexibility.*

Think of your appointments as steps along a path that may be long or short. In order to develop a path that leads to new team members or clients, it's important to listen to your prospect's needs throughout the prospecting process. New information that you hear may result in adjusting the focus of your appointment or changing the order of the next steps you'll take. Therefore, there's no guaranteed formula or pattern that will apply in the same way to every prospect.

For example, you may need to ask four times before your prospect agrees to arrange a meeting with you and your business mentor. Or your prospect may be interested in attending the BPM with nearly no effort on your part. Building skinship with your prospect usually addresses any uncertainty you have about what your prospect is looking for.

Regardless of the purpose of your appointment, you need to be able to quickly adjust to change. For instance, if, at the beginning of the appointment, your goal is to "close the deal" no matter what, you may overlook the fact that your prospect is really just looking for information before making any decisions. In the end, your pushiness may turn off your prospect. Thankfully, your business mentor will be your guide. He or she will help you decide how to continue to move forward with your prospect or whether it's time to move on to better opportunities.

Develop Measurable Results

As the popular saying goes, "What gets measured gets done." In other words, when you follow checklists, record your progress, and regularly communicate with your business mentor, you accomplish significantly more than when you skip these steps.

The more time you commit to prospecting, the faster you'll learn the art of prospecting. Remember that your business mentor will be your guide as you develop your skills. In the next chapter, you'll learn about the BPM, which is one of the most powerful resources we offer to support your prospecting efforts.

Chapter 12

Business Presentation Meeting (BPM)

Theodore Roosevelt said, "Far and away the best prize that life offers is the chance to work hard at work worth doing." In our business, you'll experience both successes and setbacks—this is true whether you're just starting or you've spent years building a solid reputation. We created the Business Presentation Meeting (BPM) to support you through the ups and downs. The BPM does the following:

1. Creates a consistent way for you to turn prospects into team members.
2. Improves the way you work.
3. Provides a continual support system to help track your progress and accomplish your goals.

In this chapter, you'll learn everything you need to know about the BPM and how to use your prospecting list to invite guests to it.

Let's Get Started! What's the BPM?

The Business Presentation Meeting (BPM) is a weekly event where you, your team members, and invited guests gather. It's a consistent and powerful place to introduce your prospects to our business, and it counts on **leverage**.

If you recall, leverage means using yourself or someone else to your greatest advantage. In Chapter 8: The Leverage Exchange, you used your business mentor's expertise to help you. The BPM is another form of leverage. In this case, you're using the expertise of leaders in the organization to support you through the BPM, and the organization is using your guests to fill the room and make the BPM a worthwhile event for everyone. A successful BPM will motivate your guests to want to follow up with you. In other words, it makes it easier to set up another appointment with your prospect. With the BPM, you have a team of many on your side: business leaders and your business mentor.

The BPM can also give you regular training and insight into successful business practices. In addition, it provides a support system and keeps you on track to meet your business goals.

Three Benefits of the BPM

A career in the financial industry gives you freedom and independence, and allows you to be your own boss. For example, you no longer have a supervisor ordering you around all day. At the same time, your success or failure is 100 percent in your hands. The BPM's role is to give you weekly support. It helps you in the following ways:

1. Increases turning prospects into team members
2. Maintains your motivation
3. Helps make your dream a reality

1. Increases Turning Prospects into Team Members

Building your team is hard work. We created the BPM to support your prospecting efforts. Think of the BPM as a weekly opportunity to grow your team. It gives you a consistent place to effectively educate your prospects. The guest-only session, which I'll describe in this chapter, excites your prospects and motivates them to want to follow up with you.

But the BPM will only work if your prospects attend it. Inviting your guests to the BPM is very similar to inviting them to any appointment. Refer to the section "Invitation Principles: How Do I Invite Prospects to an Appointment?" in the previous chapter to learn the invitation process.

2. Maintains Your Motivation

In our industry, you'll experience setbacks, rejection, and occasional failure. During these times, it's helpful to receive support from those whom you respect and trust. Every week, you'll learn ways to improve how you work.

3. Helps Make Your Dream a Reality

Imagine that you are part of a basketball team. Your team members are counting on you during games. If you refuse to attend regular team practices, your performance will suffer during the game, and your team will, too.

The BPM builds Trust and Understanding between you and your team, and it encourages you to stick to your goals. When a problem arises, you know that, without fail, your team members will be at the BPM to help you. And your team members can count on you to do the same. As a result, you remain disciplined and motivated over the long term.

The Meeting Mentality

Let's say that you ran a successful restaurant. What if, all of a sudden, you decided to close your doors whenever you felt tired or unmotivated? Your customers would certainly not be happy, and they'd probably stop coming to your restaurant. If you did the same thing often enough, you'd probably go out of business. As anyone who runs a business knows, your doors have to be open, regardless of whether or not you feel like showing up.

Your career requires a similar level of commitment. We call this a **meeting mentality**. One aspect of having a meeting mentality is that you attend BPMs and other important meetings every week. When you're determined to go to BPMs, you're telling yourself and your team that you're passionate about growing your team, sticking to your plan, staying disciplined, and reaching your professional goals. Some weeks you may be excited to attend, while others you may prefer to do any number of other things. But just as regular exercise keeps you healthy and in shape, consistently attending BPMs is a key to maintaining and improving your business.

Having a meeting mentality also means that you "lead by

example." In other words, your actions must represent what you'd like to see in others, and you should be there to support your team at every meeting. Your guests and your team members will be influenced by what you say, what you do, and how you appear. You're a role model to those around you, so take this responsibility seriously.

The Structure of the BPM

Since the BPM serves two different groups, the meeting is also split into two groups:

1. A business introduction presentation for guests
2. A team training session for everyone who is already a part of our organization

Invited guests attend a business introduction presentation, and the training session is for you and your team members. Prior to the separate guest and team training sessions, there is an icebreaking and announcements session for both guests and current team members. Here, the two groups socialize and get to know each other. The total meeting time is usually from one to two hours. Following is a typical BPM's structure:

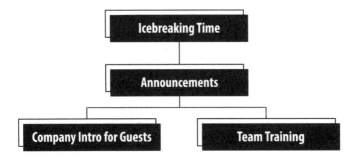

Show Your Meeting Mentality

Arrive early to BPMs. This is particularly important if you've invited a guest. His or her experience will start off in the right direction when you're there to greet your guest upon arrival. Also, make sure to dress professionally. Remember that the "B" in "BPM" stands for "Business," so dress like a businessperson. Although sayings like "Don't judge a book by its cover" mean well, appearances are very important in a business setting. Dressing well will also make you feel and look more confident.

Icebreaking and Announcements

This is the first part of the BPM. Here, team members meet with one another and socialize with their guests. After this time, team members may be recognized for their accomplishments, and you'll also hear business announcements and news.

Your job is to make your guest feel comfortable even though he or she doesn't know anyone. You want to show your guest that our business is full of friendly, hardworking people who care about each other and our organization.

Five Simple Strategies to Help Your Guest Relax

1. Do the introduction

You want your guest to feel welcome and comfortable. Therefore, don't make it your guest's job to introduce him- or herself to another person. Instead, introduce your guest to others by saying something like, "Jack, I'd like you to meet my friend Tiffany." In other words, make sure that *you* start the conversation.

2. Use your guest's background

Keep in mind that you want your guests to feel comfortable throughout the event. Part of putting them at ease is making conversations as natural and effortless as possible for them. Make sure that you introduce your guests to others rather than leaving it up to them. This is important because you don't want your guests to have to repeat the same introduction over and over—this could make them uncomfortable or cause them to view the event as boring.

If you've ever attended an event full of strangers, you've probably found yourself sharing the same details about yourself repeatedly, such as your background and what brought you to the meeting. Don't make your guest do this. Help her by saying something like, "I invited Tiffany because she wanted to learn more about us. She was born in Korea but has spent the last 15 years here."

In the previous example, the team member introduced his guest as someone who was born in Korea. Make the icebreaking sessions memorable and fun for your guests by introducing them to people with whom they may share common interests. Here are some examples:

1. Cultural and language backgrounds
2. Career and special training

3. Hobbies, interests, and special skills (sports, music, food, and more)
4. Education (schools and degrees)

3. Keep the conversation basic

While matching guests with others who share their interests is a great idea, make sure that the conversation stays friendly and warm. Avoid talking about things that may create tension. Here's where the rule about staying away from politics, sex, and religion is a good idea. There are exceptions, of course. If one person shares exactly the same religious background as someone else, he or she may be glad that you made the introduction—just be sure to use good judgment. If you're not sure, ask your business mentor.

4. Stay with your guest

It's best to be by your guest's side, even if he or she has clearly made a connection with someone else. You want your guest to know that you're glad that he or she has attended and that you're there to help.

Guest Session

After the icebreaking and announcements session, guests and team members split into two groups. During the guest session, your guests will learn about our business in a friendly setting. The presenters will share information about our business and explain some basic financial principles that will create curiosity.

The session is designed so that at the end, your guest will be excited and interested to talk to you in detail about our business.

Team Training Session

One of the most important parts of the team training session is the **"why story."** Here you and your team members share personal stories about why you are working together in our business. This is voluntary, so no one is forced to share.

You may recall that in Chapter 1: Trust and Understanding, I described the underwear story. Like the underwear story, the why story is personal and insightful. A why story should also be motivational. It can highlight things such as how you got started, the difficulties you've had, and how our business has improved your life.

During this session, you may also receive business training and hear guest speakers, and teams may provide updates regarding how their businesses are doing. The session changes to meet the needs of team members, so it may be different from week to week.

Inviting Prospects to the BPM

As I've described earlier, there's no one way to arrange an appointment. One thing, however, will always be the same: You'll always use your prospecting list as a guide. For key guidelines regarding invitations, see "Invitation Principles" in Chapter 11.

The Main Goal of the BPM: Guest Follow-Up Appointment

When you've invited a guest, the most important part of the BPM is to arrange a follow-up appointment with him or her. Let's say that you're still in the Team Training session, and you see that the guest session has ended. Your first priority is your guest, so step out of your meeting and make sure to talk to your guest before he or she leaves.

Here are three follow-up guidelines you should follow when speaking to your guests after a BPM:

1. Maintain your guest's interest.
2. Resist the urge to close immediately.
3. Plan to meet within two days.

Maintain Your Guest's Interest

Don't go into detail or spend more than a few minutes speaking to your guest. Tell her that you would like to speak to her further and set a time and date to talk. After a few minutes, politely excuse yourself and return to the meeting. For more on this, refer to the section "Appointment Setting Secret: Create Curiosity" in the previous chapter.

Resist the Urge to Close Immediately

To *close* means to get someone to commit to joining your team or becoming a client. One of the most common mistakes that new people in our business make is that they are tempted to pressure their guest to "close the deal" right away—in other words, to get the guest to become a team member or client, no matter what. They sometimes feel that if they don't act right away, the prospect will lose interest.

Because of this desperate effort to close, the guest may be given information that isn't helpful and may even be wrong, and it may turn the guest off to our business. To avoid this, remind yourself to be patient. Also, keep in mind that the goal is to set up an appointment that will include your business mentor. During your next meeting, you'll have your business mentor's support throughout the appointment.

Plan to Meet Within Two Days

Taking action right away is key. In my experience, an appointment to meet that's more than two days away has a much lower chance of happening. If there is too much time between the BPM and the meeting, the guest will usually forget why he or she was so excited and will find reasons to avoid the appointment. So do your best to schedule it within two days.

The BPM will be a significant part of your prospecting system. It's designed to motivate your prospects to want to receive additional information from you. It's also another step toward building Trust and Understanding with your prospects. Once your prospects recognize your genuine interest in their well-being, you'll often find that they'll actually *want you* to meet people they know (also called their network). Their network includes individuals whom your prospects believe will benefit from what you have to offer. These people may someday be your guests at a BPM or another type of meeting. In the next chapter, you'll learn about meetings—in addition to the BPM—that we've created to benefit you and your business. Combined, we simply call them **events**.

CHAPTER 13

Events

In addition to weekly Business Presentation Meetings (BPMs), we have larger regional and national gatherings that take place during the year. These gatherings provide powerful opportunities to grow your team and client base. In this brief chapter, you'll learn about the role of these gatherings in the life of your business.

Leverage on a Large Scale

Imagine that you were a director and you had worked for months and maybe even years on your film. You invested countless hours developing your idea, you worked hard to shoot your movie, and after filming ended, you spent weeks editing your big project. Your great work was now ready for the world to see. At your movie premiere, you're surrounded by those who supported you from the very beginning as well as your film crew and other respected people in the film industry. Invited guests have come from all over the country to celebrate with you.

Similarly, our **events** are places where we celebrate our accomplishments, meet one another, and share ideas. You'll have many opportunities to gain insight and inspiration from leaders whom you may not be able to meet with on a regular basis due to distance or a lack of time. You will also be able to leverage their combined experience and energy by taking part in our events.

We use the general term *events* to describe regional and national gatherings that our business promotes or sponsors throughout the year. The following are four different types of events:

1. Business conventions
2. Business training events
3. Team gatherings
4. Other special events

Like BPMs, your guests are welcome and are encouraged to attend events. In addition, just like BPMs, you must maintain a **meeting mentality** in order to experience the greatest benefit from events. For review, a meeting mentality is the level of commitment you show toward our business. It includes a pledge to attend events, stick to your plan, stay disciplined, and regularly work toward your professional goals.

In addition, both BPMs and events count on all participants to lead by example. In other words, your actions must represent what you'd like to see in others. Guests and team members will be influenced by what you say, what you do, and how you appear. You're a role model to those around you, so take this responsibility seriously.

Events become especially important as your team grows. This is because as you turn more prospects into team members and clients, you'll need to motivate larger groups of people, and the events provide a perfect place to host large teams. An event can bring together these large groups and motivate them in a way that you would have trouble doing on your own.

While BPMs leverage local team members, events bring together team members from different cities, counties, and states. As a result, they are powerful ways to learn how the best and brightest in our business run their teams and grow their businesses. My team members often tell me that they look forward to attending events, and for many, they are the highlight of their year. In addition, when you invite your guests to events, they'll have a great chance to see that our business is full of successful, hard-working, and friendly people from many different parts of the country. Therefore, events are a powerful way to leverage the people in our organization to increase your credibility and grow your team.

Events also show you what is possible in this business. By seeing the powerful examples of our organization's most accomplished individuals, you'll be motivated to set new and bigger goals.

As time passes and your experience deepens, you'll realize

that all top-performing team members in our organization have an ability to touch the lives of everyone they meet. They're able to do this because they've mastered building Trust and Understanding. In the next chapter, I'll explain how you, too, can develop this incredible skill. A key way to do this is to learn how to leverage your prospect list in order to create a referral system that will last the life of your career.

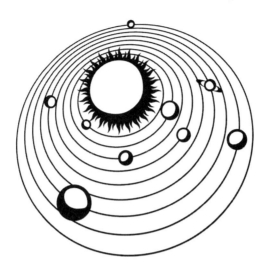

Chapter 14

Referrals

If you recall from Chapter 11, someone with a **high center of influence** is respected and known by many people. These prominent people may be pastors, community leaders, board members, teachers, principals, executives, and others with similar status or influence. Those around them trust their opinions and follow their recommendations.

When people with high centers of influence form the foundation of your prospecting list, you create nearly endless opportunities to grow your future business. In this chapter, you'll learn how to make those with high centers of influence the center of your referral system. It's a breakthrough approach that's one more benefit of focusing on Trust and Understanding.

What Are Referrals?

Referrals are recommendations you receive from people to contact someone they know. Anyone who is involved in a client-oriented business must understand that future business depends on not just our current contacts but also the people whom our contacts refer to us. In fact, these referrals are what keep our business growing. They are essential to our long-term success.

Proudly Ask for Referrals!

An important aspect of building a continual stream of prospects is relying on referrals from people who know you. But many times, people have confessed to me that they're afraid to ask for referrals. When I ask why, they share that they are fearful of hearing "No, I don't know anyone you can help," or they think it's rude to ask.

If this describes how you feel, I encourage you to take the perspective of your prospects: They've seen how hard you've worked for them, and they know you are a kind and professional individual. They've also benefitted from your commitment to creating skinship and working with your business mentor to identify their hot buttons. As a result, they appreciate the knowledge you've shared and your efforts to improve their lives.

I know this because I've experienced the gratitude of prospects. They've actually walked me to my car after our appointment and thanked me for how I've helped them. And this isn't just my experience but that of others in our business as well.

So remember this: Your grateful prospects are waiting for you to ask for referrals! They're happy to help because they want you to succeed, and they want those they care about to benefit from what you have to offer. So be bold and ask something like, "Do you know anyone I can help, as I've helped you?" When they provide you with several names, you'll be glad you took the risk, and you'll be motivated to do it again.

But if you don't like the approach I just described, you can follow a different referral method that's based on Trust and Understanding. If you are lucky, you might not have to actually "ask" for a referral ever again.

Natural Referrals

The **natural referral approach** could also be called "the world's easiest way to generate a steady stream of powerful referrals." Let's say you've spent the necessary time to truly understand and care about your prospects over the course of several appointments. As a result, you've also built Trust and Understanding. They're confident in your ability to help them, they've gained valuable insight from you, and they've expressed appreciation for your time and effort. A natural next step is that they want those they care about to benefit from what you have to offer.

At this point, it becomes easy to ask something like, "I'm glad that you've benefitted from what I've had to share. Do you know anyone else whom you think will benefit, too?" In some instances, they may be so excited about the information you've provided them that they'll give you referrals *without even having to ask!*

Thus the secret to the effectiveness of the natural referral approach is to establish enough *Trust and Understanding before you conduct business or request a referral.* This is an example of giving *before* you receive. Resist the urge to request referrals before it's appropriate. You want to have had several conversations, appointments, or both with your prospective referral source, *not just one or two interactions.*

Once the prospect has confidence in our organization and you've shown him or her the care and professionalism you have for your clients, the prospect will be happy to suggest that you reach out to people that he or she cares about to see if you can help them as well. But if you ask too early—before you've built enough trust—you might not get strong referrals, and you may also weaken opportunities for future ones.

Overall, the natural approach is the most effective way to create referrals. It's often effortless because if you build the relationships correctly, your prospects are the ones doing all the work for you. Next, you'll learn a powerful way to make your natural referral system even better.

Referrals Through Centers of Influence

Would you rather have a large group of individuals who do business with you once or a small group who give you lots of prospects but who *may never do business with you?* In other words, do you prefer *quality over quantity?*

When you have people with high centers of influence within your referral network, you're focusing on quality. By focusing your time and energy on certain prospects with high centers of influence, you can be rewarded for your efforts with a steady stream of future referrals instead of instant sales. These types of relationships take time and energy. You need to fight the temptation to "close" quickly and instead spend the time needed to truly earn the trust and admiration of those centers of influence. When they see that Trust and Understanding are the foundation of how you work, they will want you to help those they care about. As a result, they will create countless referral opportunities for you over the long term.

In addition, because of their high profiles within their communities and organizations, they'll probably know others with high centers of influence. So they are a powerful source to meet even more people with high centers of influence—the cycle can go on and on. Thus the more you build trust with people who have high centers of influence, the bigger and more effective your referral network becomes.

In addition, when those with high centers of influence refer you to their network, you'll benefit from the credibility of your referral source. These prospects will most likely trust your ability to meet their needs, so it will be easy to set up Home Visits with them rather than using other appointment methods, such as the less effective Drop-by.

Planting Seeds

On average, you should expect to have at least two to three appointments with an average prospect. But if you believe that a particular prospect has a high center of influence and you want him or her to refer people to you in the future, you might want four or five appointments to get to know him or her very well. *Think of this as planting seeds.* The seeds you plant now can grow and feed you later. A problem arises, however, when your calendar is full.

So what do you do when you're struggling to meet your current responsibilities and you have no time to think ahead? During busy times, you must regularly remind yourself that the more time you spend prospecting now, the more referral opportunities you create in the future. At this point, time management is your biggest challenge. It's time to prioritize your centers of influence.

Regardless of whether your time is free or limited, you must never lose sight of the importance of building trust, especially with those who have a high center of influence. Even if you've closed a deal with them, you should determine whether it would benefit you to continue to meet with them and build more Trust and Understanding.

When you focus on building Trust and Understanding, the natural approach should come as a logical next step in your relationship with your clients. They appreciate the time you spent helping them to improve their lives, and they see how those they care about can benefit from what you have to offer. By focusing on Trust and Understanding, you have built the foundation from which all aspects of your business benefit. While it's easy to maintain focus in the short term, keeping it up for months and years isn't. In this way, your career is more of a marathon than a sprint. In the next chapter, you'll learn how our accountability system helps keep you on track to fulfill your long-term professional goals.

CHAPTER 15

Accountability

At the core of all strong relationships is clear and regular communication. Whether it's a marriage, a business partnership, or a friendship, when people regularly express what's working well in a relationship as well as what's not, both can continually improve it. When communication breaks down, however, the connection between one person and another will suffer. In this chapter, you'll learn the system we've developed to make sure that the ties between you, your business mentor, and our business remain strong. In the end, a strong relationship between you and your business mentor will provide long-lasting benefits to your business.

Accountability Is the Key

In our business, **accountability** is the system of constant communication between you and your business mentor. Accountability strengthens koraji.

When I meet with team members every week, I'll often say, "I want accountability." By this, I mean that I want people to tell me how their businesses are progressing that week, if there are any problems, and more. Based on what they tell me, I am able to give them feedback on their specific concerns. In addition, this type of constant reporting and feedback lets me learn the koraji of my team. As a result, I can work on how to improve their businesses based on their specific strengths and weaknesses.

Accountability Keeps You on the Right Path

One of the most important reasons that you want accountability is that it strengthens your koraji. If you understand your weaknesses, accountability keeps you on the right path. If you know your strengths, it helps you make them even stronger.

There may be times when your past experiences cause you to drift from our business and training system. You may do this accidentally as a result of habits you've developed. Or you may do this on purpose because you believe that your method seems better. But once you decide to launch your new career, you've made a commitment to building Trust and Understanding. Having accountability with your business mentor is part of your promise to follow the principles of our business—even if it doesn't seem like the best approach. It's also the way we make sure that you're sticking to Basic Training.

Upgrade Your "Software"

In our business, the role of your business mentor is to help you become a master team builder and client service provider. We've created an accountability system that makes sure we're upholding the principles of Trust and Understanding. We always want to be certain that our organization and its team members are continually upgrading their skills and mindset.

Think of all your abilities like a computer's software. As you know, software, such as word processors and Internet browsers, can either slow a computer down or make it run as fast as possible. In our business, accountability ensures that if your skills and mindset need upgrading, both the organization and your business mentor are providing all the support you need. Constant communication between you and your business mentor will make certain that your skills are always up-to-date. In addition, your business mentor will improve how he or she works based on your input. So accountability benefits you *and* your business mentor. The way to continually strengthen accountability between the two of you is through skinship.

The Skinship-Accountability Connection

Accountability in our business shares traits with a strong friendship. Imagine two people who have worked hard to become best friends. In the beginning of that friendship, they probably had regular communication to get to know each other. Now imagine that one of the friends becomes really busy. As a result, the friends don't talk to one another for a couple of days. Most likely, a few days will have very little impact on the relationship. But if weeks or months pass, problems will definitely surface. Your relationship with your business mentor is similar. You've worked hard to build Trust and Understanding. But if you neglect to maintain communication with him or her, your business relationship will suffer.

Accountability runs throughout our business. You and your future team members are accountable to each other, you and your business mentor are accountable to one another, your business mentor and his or her manager are accountable to each other, and everyone and the organization itself are accountable to one another. Therefore, if one level of the accountability and communication system breaks down, the entire organization will suffer. Meanwhile, when everyone within our business follows our accountability principles, everyone benefits.

Create an Accountability System in Your Team

Following are the roles and responsibilities of you and your business mentor:

You will contact your business mentor and share about your progress on a regular basis. Using Basic Training as your guide, you should discuss the following with your business mentor:

- Your prospecting list
- Appointments you've set
- Referrals you've received
- Your questions
- Your struggles and accomplishments

Your business mentor will make him- or herself available to you. He or she is responsible for the following:

- Developing your prospect list and hot buttons with you
- Making sure that you're sticking to business goals
- Making sure that you're checking off items on your Associate Checklist
- Answering your questions
- Pointing out areas in which your business can improve and providing suggestions on how to do this

Accountability Has Many Forms

Just as there are many ways for you and your business mentor to conduct skinship and build trust, accountability is equally flexible. You can communicate with your business mentor through face-to-face conversations, phone calls, video conferencing, emails, and text messages. You'll use a combination of methods depending on the type of information you're going to share and the amount of time you and your business mentor have. With so many ways to reach out to your business mentor, you should contact him or her on a consistent basis.

Accountability Is a Constant Process

Like anything worth having in life, our business will require focus, motivation, and lots of effort. There will be times when you'll feel excited, such as after a fantastic meeting with a prospect. And there will be times when you'll experience deep frustration, such as when a prospect shows no interest in what you have to say. Accountability keeps you on track to accomplish your goals regardless of the setbacks you experience. Therefore, as you grow your business, accountability should always be at the top of your to-do list.

As I've shared throughout this book, Basic Training is your guide to launching your career and reaching your long-term goals, but success in our business *also requires mentorship*. And one of your business mentor's most important roles is to uphold accountability by making sure you're accomplishing what you set out to do. Through mentorship and accountability, you'll have the tools to maintain long-term focus and ambition.

In the next chapter, you'll learn how you and your business mentor will work together to put Basic Training into practice through building your own team. This exciting process begins with the numbers 3-3-30. These numbers will set you on the path to overcome your biggest fears, build lasting confidence, and make your career dreams a reality.

Chapter 16

Team Builder's Club

As the saying goes, "You have to learn to walk before you can run." When you start in our business, you'll most likely be very excited to experience all that your new career has to offer. But once you plunge into the everyday tasks to reach your goals, it may be difficult to maintain your enthusiasm. After all, any serious business requires hard work and sacrifice.

In order to avoid losing your focus and drive to succeed, it's important to set short-term goals in addition to your long-term ones. In fact, consistently accomplishing short-term goals will provide the continual motivation you need to achieve long-term success. In this chapter, you'll learn about our short-term goal-setting approach. We call it the **Team Builder's Club**, and it starts with the numbers **3-3-30**.

What Is 3-3-30?

The Team Builder's Club consists of people who have reached the goal of 3-3-30. These three numbers stand for the following:

- **3** business transactions and
- **3** new team members in
- **30** days

In other words, you are setting a short-term goal of having **three** new clients and **three** new team members in the next **thirty** days. We recognize individuals who achieve this goal as members of a special club that we call the Team Builder's Club. We recognize members of the Team Builder's Club on a regular basis during BPMs and events. While 3-3-30 is a minimum benchmark for recognition, many team members go far beyond 3-3-30 and gain far more clients and team members each month.

Why the Team Builder's Club?

We realize that launching your business is very difficult. You're learning a completely new way to work and think while at the same time gathering team members and clients. While you're doing everything it takes to start your business, it's easy to lose focus and become distracted. The Team Builder's Club is a goal that will make sure you're concentrating on short-term tasks that will provide the greatest long-term benefit to your business. It's also a way for your team members to acknowledge your accomplishments. In addition, it inspires them to work hard and maintain focus.

In addition, many new team members make the mistake of paying too much attention to long-term goals. Long-term goals are exciting and provide endless fuel for your imagination. You may dream of more income, nicer cars, fancier vacations, and any number of other things. Unfortunately, too much focus on goals that are far away may actually keep you from accomplishing them. This is because they may cause you to overlook the smaller steps that you need to take every day.

I've seen people fall into this trap far too many times. For instance, I'll ask someone, "What goals do you have?" An eager new team member will say, "I want to earn a very high income." But if I ask what short-term steps he's taking to accomplish this, I'll quickly see that he's not doing what's necessary *right now* to reach that bigger goal someday.

If, however, he focused on becoming a member of the Team Builder's Club in addition to his long-term goals, he would be completing everyday tasks such as building his prospect list, developing hot buttons, inviting prospects to BPMs, and arranging appointments, all of which will contribute to reaching that long-term goal.

Why 3-3-30?

We based the 3-3-30 standard on those who have experienced success in our business. We saw that when they followed our system and worked with their business mentors, they were able to gain 3 clients and 3 team members in about a month. In fact, for many team members, reaching this benchmark is a natural result of the making the Top 5 and Top 25 lists. In addition, 3-3-30 is a way to see whether you're meeting the goals that you set with your business mentor. Although 3-3-30 is no guarantee that you'll succeed, it's a strong sign that Basic Training is working for you.

Duplication

Once you become a member of the Team Builder's Club, we encourage you to duplicate your success by doing it again. However, it might be easier now because you already have three new team members who can help you meet the next 3-3-30 goal. In addition, imagine that as you continue to recruit new team members and gain new clients, you are helping and pushing your team members to do the same thing and achieve Team Builder's Club status along with you. If everyone on your team duplicates this type of success, your team grows faster—much faster—than what you could do on your own. This is where you can imagine the words "exponential growth" becoming a reality. Soon you may have more new members on your team than you thought possible.

Basic Training Prepares You for Flight

Birds aren't born flying. But once their wings are ready, they'll launch from their nests and learn to lead lives in the air. Basic Training has given you the wings to launch your new business. Now it's your job to take flight. In order to make this a lasting career, it's important to continually meet short-term goals that lead to long-term success. The Team Builder's Club is the monthly benchmark that will keep you motivated for months and years to come.

The last chapter in the Basic Training section is next. Here, I'll illustrate how everything you've learned so far will be the foundation of your long-term success.

Chapter 17

When the Student Becomes a Teacher

One of the biggest regrets I have about my career is that I wasted years of my life doing business the wrong way. One of the main drawbacks of my old way of doing business was that it lacked a system of loyalty. Those whom I recruited would leave as soon as they learned my system and better opportunities came their way. Because there was no Trust and Understanding built into our relationships, my old team members felt very little loyalty to my old organization or to me. As a result, it was difficult to grow my business while I was running that type of business system. Once I recognized the importance of Trust and Understanding, however, my ability to grow my team seemed almost limitless.

The beauty of our Basic Training system is that as you learn the steps of building your client base and team, Trust and Understanding are a natural part of how you work. Therefore, just by following our system, you are making sure that your business will benefit from Trust and Understanding. Once you master running a business based on these key principles, you'll create more opportunities to succeed.

For some of you, your next career step will be to oversee a team of your own. For others, it means managing multiple offices, managing an entire state, or beyond. The choice is yours, and you're only limited by how hard you want to work and the goals that you set for yourself.

In Chapter 9: Warm Market Prospecting, you learned about the strengths of our prospecting system:

1. It builds on leverage.
2. It is based on your koraji.
3. It's quickly learned and repeated.
4. It leads to independence.

So far, you've learned about all four of these items. The missing item that comes after "It leads to independence" is the word **duplication**. What duplication means is that you also have the ability to repeat what you've learned so you can train others and grow your team.

The Next Step: The Mindset of a Leader

When you become an expert at building one team, you have the knowledge and experience to duplicate the formula over and over again. Think of duplication as a reward you earn as a result of mastering Basic Training and hard work. Duplication is one of the most powerful benefits of following our system. In fact, we've designed our approach so that you'll always be able to expand your team and start new ones as well. There are always new and exciting opportunities waiting for you—this career is never boring!

Duplication requires you to be a leader. I use the word *leader* in the way you probably imagine: someone who heads a group of individuals. But I also use it in a way that is particular to our business.

In the next section, which is called **Leadership Training**, we'll build upon Basic Training, and you'll learn what it takes to be an amazing leader. We'll address key questions such as:

- What are the qualities and strengths that I need to head multiple teams?
- What do I need to do—every day—to ensure my team's success?
- How do I manage my limited time and resources?
- What problems will I encounter that, if not addressed correctly, could lead to disaster for my team and me?
- How do I organize my team?

And more.

You'll learn the qualities that leaders must have in order to successfully build one team and duplicate the formula to build another. We've made the formula as easy to understand as we can. The bottom line is that being a leader isn't complicated, but it does require you to be patient and follow our leadership approach. Just as in Basic Training, there's no room to "reinvent the wheel" or skip steps. If you decide to follow your own path, you'll create unnecessary roadblocks that will get in the way of accomplishing your goals and that can even lead to failure.

In the end, Leadership Training cannot work without first mastering Basic Training. But Basic Training without Leadership Training will limit what you'll be able to accomplish. If your plan is to become a respected leader who heads a large team, Leadership Training is for you.

With focus, hard work, and a track record of accomplishments, you'll one day master the principles of leadership. At the same time, one of the most important qualities of the best leaders is that they are *always* learning more, earning the loyalty of others, and inspiring others to do their best. By maintaining focus and discipline, your leadership skills will continue to improve.

So get ready to be part of a Leadership Business master class. If you've been waiting for the tools to skyrocket your career, then read on...you won't be disappointed.

Part 3

Leadership Training

CHAPTER 18

Leaders Are Created, Not Born

With your business mentor's guidance, you learned the principles of Trust and Understanding. The combined efforts of you and your business mentor resulted in your ability to make our business system a key part of how you run your business. By working together, you began building your team and business in a way that you'd eventually be able to duplicate on your own. When you reach the duplication stage, it means that you're ready to think about your career differently than you have up to this point. In fact, you now need to think as a leader rather than as a student. In the next two chapters, you'll learn our leadership fundamentals. I'll describe the *three ways that Trust and Understanding apply to leadership, the three qualities of top leaders,* and *three techniques that will make you a great leader.*

Why Is Leadership Important?

Imagine if you asked someone, "Would you like a career in which you could experience professional and financial freedom?" Most people would answer with an enthusiastic "Yes." But in reality, this dream isn't for everyone. Even those who have a strong wish to be successful may not have the drive or motivation to develop the required ownership mentality.

One reason for this has to do with our backgrounds. We all come from different places, mindsets, and circumstances, and these play a large role in whether we will succeed or fail in our careers. At the same time, I truly believe that if a person puts all of his or her energy into following our system, he or she can overcome nearly any self-limiting belief or circumstance and experience career success. I've seen it over and over. People from a wide range of life experiences and cultures have been able to triumph over what would seem like the impossible. In fact, if you're looking for success stories to motivate your team, you'll find plenty within our organization. We have countless examples that will encourage you and your team to push yourselves.

With that said, it's not always easy to identify whether the newest member of your team will succeed. Basic Training is designed to give everyone on your team the essentials they need to do well in this business. At that point, it's your responsibility to teach them our system and ensure that they stick to it. You can do this by following our approach, being a positive example, and inspiring and motivating your **team**.

By **team**, I'm referring to individuals whom you've invited to work with you as your team members. You may have started in our business without any experience being in charge of a team. Or you may have years of experience leading others in different jobs or roles. Regardless of your background, it's important to realize that in our organization, leadership means that you're open to new ways of thinking and working. If you're convinced that you have nothing left to learn or that leadership isn't that important, it's time to rethink your point of view. Otherwise, you're putting your ability to reach your goals at risk.

Newcomers often wonder why we emphasize the importance of being a leader so much. The thinking goes like this: If I can build my business on my own and maintain it by myself, why bother learning a leadership system? But people who have this perspective quickly learn that without leadership—and our approach to it—their businesses are impossible to maintain. For proof, you need only look at other financial services companies.

The survival rate for those starting in the financial services industry as a whole is very low. I have seen countless examples of high turnover in other companies I have worked with.

Typically, eager new team members started the training process, and the companies that hired them spent lots of time and money teaching them about products, services, and sales strategies. Despite investing a tremendous amount of resources on these newcomers, the organizations knew that most would fail. In fact, I believe that over 80 percent of new recruits in the rest of the industry quit before finishing their first year. The sad fact is that these companies often recruit as many people as possible, predicting that most would leave and only a few would continue.

Within these other companies, newly trained recruits are filled with lots of classroom knowledge, but they often do not get enough real-world skills that are needed in order to survive. It's as if they were taught a new language by reading books and listening to teachers, and after a few weeks they were expected to walk outside and communicate fluently with native speakers.

I found this formula for failure both heartbreaking and unacceptable. That's why I'm so proud of the completely different approach our organization takes to training our team members. Our method gives new team members an ideal combination of instruction *and* hands-on experience. Through the guidance and time investment that leaders like you provide, those entering our business are set up to succeed.

Our training has an emotional part as well. Team members see our commitment to their well-being and realize how we pour our hearts into meeting their needs. This is an important part of building Trust and Understanding, and I'm sure that your firsthand experience with this played a role in your decision to join our organization. Now that you're a leader, it's your turn. This is your opportunity to transfer the principles of Trust and Understanding to everyone on your team.

The Three Ways That Trust and Understanding Apply to Leadership

In previous chapters, you've learned the role that Trust and Understanding play in your overall business. Now you'll learn the specific role that Trust and Understanding play in leadership. This is the most important part of being a leader. Making Trust and Understanding the foundation of how you lead requires the following:

1. Having an ownership mentality
2. Following our teamwork approach
3. Believing in our business system

You must have all three of these in order to lead your team. If you're missing one or more, you can certainly develop whatever skill you lack. But until you do, you won't succeed.

1. An Ownership Mentality

When people first start in our organization, they may think of themselves as employees rather than as businesspeople. This is normally the case for the majority of those who have never run a business. After all, if you haven't run one before, it's nearly impossible to know what it's like. But the bottom line is: *Rather than thinking of yourself as an employee working at a job, you must believe and act as if you're running a business.* Thankfully, by following our system, you'll have everything you need to take on this role with confidence. I believe that nearly anyone can have an ownership mentality by putting aside any self-limiting beliefs and working hard to reach his or her professional goals. In fact, one of the most fulfilling parts of training new team members is to see someone develop an ownership mentality when he or she didn't have one before.

2. Teamwork

In our business, your success depends on the accomplishments of those on your team. In other words, unlike the way most people work in other organizations, in our organization *you can't succeed by yourself.* To use an example from sports, your role is more like a baseball pitcher than a tennis player. In tennis, you're the only one who will win or lose on the court. In baseball, however, your role as the pitcher may be important, but without your team members' efforts, you'll never win.

You've counted on others to teach you our system and help you grow your team, and you'll continue to depend on your colleagues and business mentors for years to come. Now that you're in charge of a team, you must think of yourself as a leader with people counting on you. And as you grow, you'll be responsible for multiple teams.

3. A Belief in the Business System

I'm a firm believer in making every business concept as simple as possible. It's the way I work best, and it's a formula that has led to the success of thousands of people just like you. Thus our system is easy to understand and memorize, and is ready for you to duplicate. In order to be an effective leader, you have to believe in the system of business that we've developed. You have to trust that it's effective and that it can improve the lives of others. Otherwise, you will spend most of your energy "reinventing the wheel" instead of duplicating and growing your team.

An Underwear Story About Leadership

Before I discovered our current approach to leading a team, I was filled with confusion and frustration. I knew that I was good at what I did, and I was proud of my skills. At the same time, communication was a major obstacle. My team members weren't following through with my instructions, and my overall frustration with them was growing.

I thought to myself, "Why aren't my team members performing better? All I see is laziness and an inability to follow simple directions." My team members were certainly smart enough to take care of their responsibilities. So when they'd ask me the same basic questions over and over, I believed that all they needed to do was work harder and manage their time better—it was that simple. But no matter how many times I told them this, I wouldn't see any improvement.

At the same time, I knew that they were just as unhappy with me as I was with them. While I saw them as lazy and disorganized, I'm sure they viewed me as difficult and impatient.

My Leadership Reality Check

You've probably heard the saying, "When the student is ready, the teacher will come." It's often at our lowest points when someone comes to us with a solution.

I was first introduced to Jack through one of my business networks. The moment we met, I instantly knew he had a talent for understanding people. As we got to know each other, we both shared about our backgrounds. He had spent years earning advanced degrees in psychology and helping others, and he could see that I was unhappy with my situation. He asked me to explain why, and he listened to my complaints. Finally he said, "I think there's a simple solution to your big problem."

His observation caught my attention. "What is it?" I asked.

"I don't think you're listening enough," he said.

When I asked him to clarify, he explained that it was obvious that I was good at what I did. The problem was that I wasn't able to transfer my knowledge to others. I was telling them what I *wanted* them to learn instead of telling them what *they* *needed* to learn. According to him, fixing this problem was as simple as listening more and talking less. That would allow me to figure out what I needed to teach.

For the first time, someone pointed out that perhaps my team members weren't completely lazy, unfocused, or both. Perhaps part of the problem was that I wasn't doing a good job of listening to them. And without listening, I didn't know what they needed, so any solution I gave would most likely be unhelpful.

By knowing my weaknesses and having a desire to change, I listened more, talked less, and used Trust and Understanding as the foundation of everything I did—and I couldn't have imagined a better result. The communication block between my team members and me dissolved. It was as if I had been wearing earplugs for years, and they were finally removed. Suddenly I was able to understand their problems with more clarity than I ever had before, and I was able to provide them with tools to figure things out.

Meanwhile, my team appreciated my insights. They knew that I cared about them, and they worked hard to overcome obstacles they faced. We were accountable to one another and committed to reach common goals together. I learned how to figure out what they needed, and they appreciated my efforts to help them.

Jack helped me realize that my ego was not only getting in the way of my success, but it was also creating the circumstances for professional failure. My ego told me that I was right, and for me that meant everyone else was wrong. The thought that my team could actually teach me something had been completely absurd. But over time, I began to see that my team members could be my teachers. They pointed out where my weaknesses were. And by being completely honest and open, I was able to see areas where I needed to grow. I realized that my understanding of being a leader needed to be completely reexamined. In the next chapter, I'll explain some of the strategies and techniques that can help you upgrade—in other words, improve—your leadership ability.

Chapter 19

Leadership Strategy

What is a leader? At its most basic level, a leader is someone who can run a business and duplicate that process with new team members. As I shared earlier, this is a huge responsibility because many who enter our business have no prior experience in the financial services industry, and they've never run their own business.

Becoming a leader is one point along a path that will stretch the entire length of your career. In fact, you can think of it as the beginning of a new and exciting journey. As you've learned, in this business we emphasize that you must have an ownership mentality. Having an ownership mentality means that you must also accept the fact that you'll always have lots of competition ready to take your place in the event that you become careless, lazy, or both. Thus you must continually develop your strengths, overcome your weaknesses, and push yourself. Clearly, the rewards of having an ownership mentality are great, but like all things worth having in life, you'll have to work hard.

The Qualities of Top Leaders

We've identified the following three key qualities that leaders should have in order to grow and continue to stand apart from others in the industry:

1. Lifelong learning
2. Servant leadership
3. Humility

1. Lifelong Learning

The moment you stop learning, your business is dead. To avoid this, you must always maintain what's called a "beginner's mind." This means that regardless of how many years of experience you have, you believe that there's always something new waiting for you to learn. You view your colleagues, clients, team members, and business mentors as your guides just as much as you are theirs. And when it comes to challenges, you'll view them as learning opportunities.

As I described in my story about leadership, at one point in my career I lost sight of the "beginner's mind." My years of hard work and discipline, as well as countless hours of self-study, convinced me that no one could teach me anything I hadn't heard or read about already. At the same time, I was unsatisfied, my actions were causing others unhappiness, and I was frustrated with my career. Worst of all, I didn't know what to do.

Fortunately, I met someone who reminded me to have a beginner's mind. Jack made me realize that—despite my accomplishments—I still had a lot to learn. But rather than take his observations as bad news and give up, I decided to do whatever was necessary to overcome my weaknesses. Therefore, I plunged into even more self-study and continued to develop my team-building skills. What started off as a feeling of despair turned into inspiration that led to a team-building approach that has improved many lives. I also learned a valuable lesson—*learning never stops.*

This industry is very competitive. Organizations often steal business-building secrets from one another. My colleagues constantly ask me, "Aren't you afraid that our competitors will one day take the Trust and Understanding formula and duplicate it in their companies?" But I'm not afraid of that.

There will always be someone who is smarter and more talented than me, but I'm convinced that *no one will work harder.* No matter how many ideas others take from me, I'll always be ahead because I'm constantly creating new ways to grow and be a better leader. I encourage you to maintain the same attitude.

2. Servant Leadership

People in our business often wonder why I work so hard. If I've learned to count on others through teamwork, shouldn't I have less responsibility, not more? But it seems as though the more our business grows, the more I'm working seven days a week. Part of it has to do with the fact that I love what I do. I could probably get away with working less... in fact, I'm sure I could. But I'm passionate about continually improving our team-building approach, inspiring others to reach their fullest potential, and helping them to understand our business. This last point—helping others understand our business—describes **servant leadership**.

One of the most important roles you play in your team members' lives is that of someone who meets their needs. For instance, I still perform PFCs despite the fact that I'm running a business and many other highly qualified people could take care of this. But if I believe that a particular client or team member will benefit from my role in the PFC, I'll make the time to be there. This is one example of many that illustrate that no matter how high your position within the organization, you should always be ready to serve others.

Servant leadership extends not only to those whom you recruited but to the broader team as well, which includes nearly everyone involved in the organization. It means that you've built trust with your team members. So when they need your guidance, you'll know exactly what solutions to provide.

As you lead your team, you do so knowing that it's your responsibility to understand all aspects of your business, to know your team's strengths and weaknesses, to support your team members, and to put their needs before yours. Although you have more experience and knowledge than your team members, you choose not to control your team members' actions. Yes, you give them the tools to succeed, but you don't interfere with their ability to learn from their own mistakes.

3. Humility

No matter how successful you become in our business, you must always view yourself as equal—never superior—to everyone in the organization. You may have more skills and experience than those around you, but you must never think that any task is too small or beneath you. This connects with the ownership mentality. *You need to do whatever it takes to get the job done.*

Imagine that you own a restaurant. You walk outside your business one day and see a pile of trash by the entrance. The last thing you want to do is sweep up the litter. At the same time, you're ready to do what it takes to ensure that your business is operating at its best. In addition, your actions inspire those around you to follow your example. So, despite your long to-do list, you grab a broom and clean up the mess.

Humility also means that you listen more than you talk. Most people are good at one-sided communication. In other words, they are good at hearing the sound of their own voices. But effective communication requires you to listen to others more than you speak.

Unfortunately, many are so eager to "sell" to their prospects that they don't take the time to figure out what the other person truly needs. By listening first, you'll figure out their hot buttons and will be able to provide solutions that address their particular concerns.

Finally, humility means that you always maintain the attitude that you aren't special, and neither is anyone on your team. Does that sound harsh? Let me explain.

Imagine that you enrolled in a math class. The first day of school, you're sitting with your fellow students when the teacher enters the room. The moment you see her, you raise your hand and say the following:

"Ms. Instructor, let me tell you how I learn best and then share what I'd like to learn in your class." Of course, you probably would not behave in such an arrogant and disrespectful way. Behavior like that would definitely doom you to failure. *But for some reason, some people walk into our business with that same attitude.*

Being a good leader means that you don't expect others to treat you a certain way simply because of your status or accomplishments. Of course, you should be proud and confident about what you've achieved. But you should always balance your successes with a belief that you expect to receive the same amount of respect that you give others.

Techniques That Will Help Make You a Great Leader

So far, you've learned the three ingredients that make Trust and Understanding the heart of how you lead. Next, you've learned three qualities of top leaders. Now you'll learn how to be an effective leader.

Being a great leader requires you to work every day to improve your team members' lives as well as your team's overall performance. You can meet these goals by doing the following:

1. Knowing the koraji of your team members
2. Applying people skills that are rooted in Trust and Understanding
3. Motivating and inspiring your team

1. Knowing the koraji of your team members

Unless you know the koraji of your team members, you can't possibly apply Trust and Understanding to motivate and inspire your team.

You've already been introduced to koraji in terms of how it applies to your relationship with your mentor. In Basic Training, I explained that you and your mentor counted on skinship and ssagaji. Now it's your turn to be a mentor. Skinship is key to being a great mentor, and there's no substitute for it. Regardless of how busy you become and how limited your time is, you must continue to make skinship one of your top priorities. In the next chapter, you'll learn how to balance skinship with the enormous responsibilities you have as a leader.

If you've invested time in skinship, you know your team members' koraji. And as you've already learned, skinship requires ssagaji. Through skinship, you'll know the degree to which individuals on your team are motivated to succeed. For example, you'll be able to determine whether their motivation is weak or strong. You also understand each team member's strengths and weaknesses. As a result, you understand the strengths and weaknesses of your entire team. Armed with this valuable information, you're able to ask others in the organization for specific help because you know exactly where your team needs to improve. When you approach every connection with a team member keeping koraji in mind, you've built a team based on Trust and Understanding.

2. Applying people skills that are rooted in Trust and Understanding

Ours is a people business. This means that your and your team's ability to connect with others is key to your business's success. You may have tons of product knowledge and financial expertise far beyond everyone else, but without people skills your business won't grow. In addition, you may have great people skills, but if members of your team don't, your business won't grow. Thus, you need to be able to teach yourself *and others* about developing people skills.

What do good people skills look like? And if you don't have them, how do you develop them? Lastly, how do you transfer your people skills to your team?

Solid people skills require you to be a great listener. Rather than jump right into providing solutions, whether it's to your prospects or current team members (I'll call these people your **audience**), you need to first know what problems your audience has.

If you recall from my underwear story about leadership, I thought I was a good listener. What I learned, however, was that I was really good at providing answers that perhaps my audience didn't need. I was full of product and career knowledge. *But because I wasn't able to touch the hearts and minds of my audience, my knowledge wasn't helping them.* Once I learned to truly listen to others, I was able to use my knowledge in new and powerful ways.

And by listening, I'm also including what is *not said,* which is usually called **body language**. What are the expressions on the person's face telling you? Is she happy, sad, excited, or depressed? How is her posture: upright or slumped over? Understanding people's body language is just as important as understanding what they say. That's why we emphasize face-to-face interactions with your prospects rather than phone calls, emails, and text messages. Those forms of communication should only play a supporting role in your connection to others.

For example, let's say that one of your team members is meeting with a potential team member, and both of you have identified that one of her hot buttons is that she wants to earn more money. When your team member meets with her, he shares about the income opportunities that this business offers. Despite his best efforts, she isn't convinced.

Your team member later shares that the prospect wants to earn more money so she can send her kids to college. Suddenly, new opportunities to build Trust and Understanding emerge. The next time you meet, you provide the prospect with specific solutions based on her children's educational timelines. Rather than just talk about what this business offers, you listen closely to her needs and then push her to shift her thinking. You show her that she does not have a lot of time to create a more stable financial future for her kids. She appreciates that you learned about her situation and addressed her biggest fears. As a result, she believes that joining your team will provide her the financial help that she's looking for.

"Reading" people (or determining their thoughts based on what they say and don't say) takes practice. You need to do this over and over—thousands of times—with different people. With enough experience with different people, you'll become an expert at people skills, which will be invaluable both in your own prospecting efforts and in training your team.

There's no substitute for practicing people skills in the real world beyond classrooms and how-to books. After all, if everyone who wanted to improve his or her people skills could do it by reading a book, we'd have a lot more expert communicators. You and your team can find endless information in books and on the Internet about how to improve people skills, and they may provide valuable insights. But the key word in "people skills" is *people*. Unlike "math skills" or "writing skills," you can't develop people skills without talking to others. *No amount of self-study or classroom learning can substitute for going out and meeting as many people as possible.* By watching and listening, you learn how individuals think and react to information.

3. Motivating and inspiring your team

In our business, we believe that motivation and inspiration are both important, but we define them differently.

Motivation provides *short-term* benefits, and **inspiration** provides *long-term* ones. While both require knowing your team members' koraji, there are differences between the two.

To motivate means that you provide your team with brief bursts of encouragement to move them forward. This career, like anything else worth having, requires intense focus and commitment. At some point in your team members' careers, they'll most likely go through days, weeks, or even months when they feel frustrated. During these tough times, they'll count on their colleagues to help them through the ups and downs.

The BPM is an example of a motivational tool. BPMs happen once a week. During these short meetings, team members share their success stories and push one another to continue to stay focused and work hard until the next meeting. As a leader, you want to encourage those on your team to share about their growth during BPMs. Thus it's important to be a careful observer of your team members. Being able to spot a motivating story requires that you know each team member's koraji. Part of being a good leader means that you're aware of those on your team who are changing and growing. Keep an eye on these rising stars on your team and, when it's time, have them share their experiences.

When we hold major events where people from all over the country gather, we'll often have a motivational speaker give a talk. While it's a nice change to have someone from outside our business address the audience, I'm fully convinced that there are endless numbers of people *within* our organization who have powerful stories to tell. When you realize this, you'll find yourself with endless sources for motivating your team.

Although motivation is a great way to encourage one another, its effect may not last very long. Team members may leave an event, like a BPM, full of energy and excitement, but their motivation may quickly fade away. Enter the role of **inspiration**.

Providing **inspiration** to your team is about driving them forward over the long term. In order to inspire your team, you must know the following:

1. Their long-term goals
2. Their fears
3. Their hopes
4. Their strengths
5. Their weaknesses

Where motivation is more of a "one size fits all" approach, such as a powerful speech given to a group of people, inspiration is custom and personal. Every team member is inspired by something different.

Imagine that you had a team member who told you he wanted to make more money. If you hadn't bothered to learn more, you wouldn't know exactly what inspired him.

Instead, you were wise enough to ask something like, "What

are your biggest hopes?" and he responded, "Providing opportunities for my kids that I never had." Now you have the information necessary to inspire him. When he's feeling frustrated, you can remind him of his longer-term goal of helping his children. When he loses focus, you can remind him why he joined your team in the first place.

This example points to how inspiring your team members is a significant time commitment. By figuring out what inspires each team member, you'll know who to focus your limited time and energy on. For example, you'll want to aim your resources on team members who have strong reasons to be part of your team versus weak ones.

Those with an unstoppable drive to succeed will do whatever it takes to show up to BPMs, schedule PFCs, and learn how to build Trust and Understanding. These hard-working individuals have big dreams and are willing to make the sacrifices and put forth the effort to accomplish their goals. Therefore, they will play a central role in the success of your team. Not only are you helping them overcome obstacles and reach their career objectives, but inspiration also means that you're pushing them to set bigger and better goals for themselves.

The Fast Track to Leadership

In our business, leaders are created, not born. We don't believe that you need any special abilities to be a powerful leader. In fact, we believe that almost anyone can be a great one. By following our system, you'll lead with confidence, you'll earn the respect of your team members, and you'll improve the lives of countless people.

When you put aside your ego and follow our approach, you've brought yourself closer to the goal of leading not just one team but multiple teams. We've designed our leadership system so you can duplicate your formula for success many times throughout your career. Duplication takes time management and concentration, which both become very difficult to maintain as your business grows. Thankfully, we've "been there, done that." We know the challenges you'll face and the ways to address them. In the next chapter, you'll learn how to identify highly motivated individuals who will benefit your team most. By focusing on these team members, you're also managing your time wisely. Next, I'll describe our system of organizing your team.

Chapter 20

The 7 Point List

Running a team (or many teams) is a huge responsibility. It means that you're always busy, you're always looking for ways to duplicate your success, and you're constantly inspiring your team members.

In order to keep your business running smoothly, you need to be a great leader. Leadership done right takes hard work and solid time-management skills. But no matter how good you are at juggling the multiple roles you play, sometimes the duties of being a leader will overwhelm you. Fortunately, our system is here to help. We've developed tools to help you work efficiently.

By following our system, your entire team will have our time-management approach built in. For instance, knowing the koraji of your team members means that you know whom to count on based on your team members' particular strengths. In addition, because teamwork is based on Trust and Understanding, your team shares a desire to meet common goals. In this chapter, you'll learn the next step in building your team. The 7 Point List takes koraji and gives you a way to use it to improve your time management. You'll learn our powerful approach to evaluating the mindset of your team members. You'll count on this list over and over throughout your career.

Time Management and Your Team

There's only one of you. But, as you've learned, being a leader means that you're playing multiple roles. Although the rewards of success are great, you'll no doubt have to manage your time wisely to achieve your dreams.

So how do you meet the demands of so many people on a regular basis? And how do you ensure that you're focusing your limited resources on those who will contribute the most to your team? The simple solution is that you need to spend more time with certain team members and less with others. And the team members you should focus on the most are those who have the greatest potential for growth. The 7 Point List will be your guide in managing your precious time.

What Is the 7 Point List?

The list helps you answer the basic question "How much do I want to work with this particular person?" Remember, you must think of yourself as a businessperson rather than a company employee, which means that you need to think of your team members as business partners. Thus you want to surround yourself with those who share your commitment to hard work and doing business the right way.

Next, the list helps you answer the question "How much of my limited time and resources should I commit to a particular person?" We developed the 7 Point List to help you determine who will be the most important players on your team. You'll use this information to manage your time wisely.

Skinship and Koraji Lead to the 7 Point List

You'll be a business mentor to your team members as they go through Basic Training, which means that for the next few weeks, you'll be investing time in skinship with new team members. Through skinship, you'll get to know one another's koraji—and koraji is how you'll address each item on the 7 Point List.

The 7 Point List helps you figure out the growth potential of each individual team member. With that said, meeting the criteria of each item on the list doesn't guarantee, with 100 percent certainty, that a particular team member will succeed. Similarly, not meeting certain items on this list isn't a formula for failure—as long as you and your team members are continually improving.

The 7 Point List is an effective way to figure out each team member's mindset and potential growth. In general, not all seven points must be met, but the more the better. We recommend that your team members meet four or more of the list's items. Those who meet four or more points are most likely to work hard, accomplish what they set out to do, help your entire team to grow, and be a pleasure to work with. This doesn't mean that you give up on people who meet less than four items. But it does mean that as your team and your to-do list grow, the 7 Point List will help you manage your limited time wisely.

Your Team Members' "Score" Can Change

It's important that the 7 Point List be used as a guide that you keep in mind as you build trust and spend time with your team members. But avoid treating it as a one-time questionnaire during which you literally read each item to your team members and record their responses. Instead, you want to study this list, memorize it, and keep it in mind as you learn each team member's koraji. Thus, rather than being a one-time test, such as in the case of a driver's license or citizenship test that you take once and have only one opportunity to pass or fail, the results of the 7 Point List will continually change. In fact, you'll be amazed and impressed at how our system inspires your team members to continually push themselves and improve in areas where they were weak.

Furthermore, through skinship, the answers to each item on the 7 Point List will naturally emerge. So, if someone were to ask how many items on the list a particular team member met, you'd know exactly how to answer without the team member even knowing that the list existed.

The 7 Point List has the following items:

> **7 Point List**
>
> 1. Positive Attitude
> 2. Book of Business
> 3. Leadership Quality
> 4. Stable Income
> 5. Coachable
> 6. Dissatisfied
> 7. Ambition

In the next section, you'll learn the key parts of each item.

1. Positive Attitude

A great attitude has three parts: **care**, **humility**, and **kindness**. Let's explore each of them.

Care has two aspects:

1. Your team members want what's best for their clients and their fellow team members.
2. Your team members aren't 100 percent motivated by money.

Like any career, an important reason to join this business is to earn money. But this profession is about more than just experiencing financial rewards. It's about experiencing psychological ones as well. While closing deals is critical, this should never be the *only* reason your team members work. They must also have a desire to improve the lives of others. They must have a genuine interest in helping them to succeed. They want the entire team to reach its goals, and they want their clients to make better financial decisions. If they do not have this attitude, they will probably take shortcuts and do business the wrong way.

Next is **humility**. Remember, this business requires your team members to shift their thinking. Rather than consider themselves as employees of a company, they must have an ownership mentality. This means that the future of the team is in their hands, so no task is beneath them. Thus all meetings are important, as is showing up on time to them, and no matter how much knowledge a team member has, there's always something new to learn.

Even if one of your team members thinks her approach is better, she sticks to the system. In addition, humility has to do with servant leadership. Regardless of the amount that your team member accomplishes, she's always willing to do whatever it takes to meet the needs of her team.

The third part of a positive attitude is **kindness**. Your team members are always respectful toward their team members and clients. They are "team players," which means that they try hard to get along with the entire team. They treat others with respect. These people support others as they work to meet their goals, and they realize that the help they offer others won't always provide an immediate financial benefit. In fact, at times they'll sacrifice self-interest for the sake of benefitting the entire team.

A **positive attitude** is the most important of all seven items on this list. Without the three parts of a positive attitude—

care, **humility**, and **kindness**—your team members can't build Trust and Understanding. While some of us can reach short-term success in the absence of a positive attitude, long-term success requires it.

2. Book of Business

One purpose of the 7 Point List is to help you figure out the individuals who will grow the fastest and benefit your team the most. The book of business is a way to determine who your top business partners will be.

On one hand, your team members may join your team having lots of prior product knowledge and years of experience in the financial services industry. On the other hand, if they don't know anyone and don't work hard to increase their network, they'll most likely experience little success.

When you think about your team members, you need to ask yourself, "Who on my team has the strongest contact list?" As you've learned, the best lists include individuals with high centers of influence, which means that you want to concentrate on team members who have a high-quality list of people who will refer business to them.

In addition, you want to encourage your team members to expand how they view their book of business. Let's say that one of your team members is a real estate agent. When she reviews her contacts, she may think of her network in terms of home buyers and sellers. It's your job to help her to look at her list in a new way. You'll encourage her to determine how her contacts will benefit from her new career. As a result, her list goes from being filled with home buyers and sellers to one that's made up of people who know many other people. Her list is now filled with new opportunities to talk to centers of influence.

3. Leadership Quality

Plenty of people say they want to be successful in business, but to actually make their words a reality requires hard work and doing everything needed to succeed. It's essential that you and your team members have an ownership mentality. After all, if you want your team to grow, you need individuals who are willing to become leaders.

Imagine that Paul is a restaurant owner. His Chinese restaurant has succeeded because of its famous kung pao chicken. Suddenly, another Chinese restaurant opens up next door. Within weeks, Paul loses 50 percent of his business. He goes next door to see what his competition is up to. Not only does the new restaurant serve kung pao chicken, but it also has five other dishes that Paul's restaurant doesn't. He asks his chefs to come up with new dishes for the restaurant. But the chefs are afraid of creating new recipes. They don't want to be fired if the new dishes aren't popular. So they ignore Paul and don't follow his recommendation. Months later, business is so bad that he is forced to shut down his restaurant.

Fear of "stepping up" (fear of taking responsibility and following through with what's best for your team) is a quality that you don't want your team members to have. Instead, you want team members who are willing to take chances and seize opportunities to help the organization as well as their own business.

Team members who have an ownership mentality are hard working, self-motivated, and ready to learn new things, and they follow through with their commitments. They're always willing to take on any task if it will benefit the entire team. You want people who are constantly looking for ways to improve their own lives and the lives of those around them. You want team members who will seek out help when they need it and who are eager to support others on your team.

In addition, Leadership Quality includes **servant leadership**. You learned about this in the previous chapter. A servant leader is ready to put others' needs before her own, and she realizes that helping others is one of the most important roles she can play.

4. Stable Income

Although this item is titled Stable Income, we could also call it Stable Life because quality of income and quality of life often work together. This isn't to say that having lots of money guarantees a stable life. But not having money is a formula for an unstable one. Thus we want individuals who have a stable income, which is a good indicator of overall well-being.

Because you and your team members must think of yourselves as businesspeople rather than as employees of a company, you must also recognize that this has an impact on income as well. If you're an independent businessperson, you must realize that the initial investment of time and energy into your organization means that you probably won't earn income right away. Meanwhile, if you were hired to be an employee, you'd expect to receive your first paycheck on the company's official payday.

In this business, your team members must expect that they will at first receive little or no income as they establish themselves. This may not necessarily be the case. We have plenty of stories of new team members earning money almost immediately after joining our business. But practicing Trust and Understanding requires honesty about possible scenarios that your team members may encounter. Thus most shouldn't expect to earn money from day one in their new career.

We encourage you to recruit people who currently have some sort of income or financial support. A stable income indicates that a potential team member is a good planner. It shows that he or she isn't jumping into this career out of desperation. Furthermore, it's very hard to change careers when a person has no money. For example, how will a potential team member attend meetings and appointments if he or she can't afford car payments or even gas? How will a new team member cover costs for his or her licensing requirements?

5. Coachable

If you recall from Chapter 19: Leadership Strategy, I provided the example of a math student on the first day of school. Imagine that he raised his hand and told his instructor, "I'm going to tell you how I learn best and what I expect to learn in this class." This would be absurd. But I've had team members say, "This is how I am, and I want to learn this and that." This type of mindset usually doesn't work out well for the team member or for his or her team.

This business requires you to drop your ego when it's getting in the way. Our ego can be our best friend or our worst enemy. It can push us to overcome obstacles or keep us locked into habits that are holding us back. An ego can insist that we do things a certain way, even if it's not working out for us. We may have opportunities to learn new skills, but our ego keeps us from opening our mind.

Allow me to illustrate. Think of a coachable person as a sponge. The team member soaks up new information and approaches as a sponge absorbs water. In other words, whatever tools you give her, she eagerly accepts them. It seems that her desire to learn and help others is endless. She eagerly attends BPMs and PFCs because she knows that she'll either receive or give helpful information. And she is committed to following Basic Training.

Then there's an uncoachable person. This individual is more like a rock. No matter what you pour on him, he doesn't absorb it. In fact, he pushes it away. You could be giving him career-changing advice, and he may listen, but he won't take any action. Your investment of time and care is a complete waste because he refuses to take on new approaches. *The bottom line is that you want sponges, not rocks.*

6. Dissatisfied

Many of us are motivated by the pursuit of pleasure. We look forward to the reward that lies ahead. But unhappiness is often a powerful motivator as well. In this case, your team member will do whatever it takes to escape an unhappy situation. If she were completely satisfied with her life, she'd most likely not be very motivated to change her current circumstances and work hard.

Your team members may be tired of the boxed life. If you recall, this phrase describes the routine that many adults follow: Wake up, go to work, go home, and repeat. In a boxed life, the only reason to work is to earn a paycheck. Your team member may find herself wanting more out of her unsatisfying job, she may want to get rid of debt, she may have anxieties about the future, or all three.

Fortunately for her, you come along and provide her with an alternative to the present unhappiness and fears about the future that she feels. She may not have known that there was a way out of the boxed life until you presented her with new opportunities.

But before you offer an alternative to the boxed life, you must first identify the source of her dissatisfaction. By investing time in skinship, you'll know your team's koraji. Maybe she wants to spend more time with her family, but her current job doesn't allow it. Or perhaps she wants to earn additional income to pay for her children's college educations. Whatever the case, koraji will tell you what kind of life your team member envisions for herself. As a result, you'll be able to help her in her search for new opportunities. You'll use her koraji to answer questions such as:

- What about your team member's current job would he or she like to improve?
- What aspects of your team member's life are making him or her unhappy?
- Where does your team member see his or her life in five years?

Most people don't have clue about their future. The **vision stretch** is a way to push your team to think about the direction they'd like their lives to take. It helps motivate these people to see beyond their boxed lives and into a future full of promise.

What makes a person dissatisfied with his or her current situation may not be something as easy to identify as "I want to earn more money," or "I hate my job and can't wait to start something new!" Discontent may have to do with things that aren't directly related to wanting to earn more money or have a better job title. Perhaps your team member already has a career that pays well. But he's looking for more professional fulfillment. He wants a career that excites him and one that will give him the opportunity to improve the lives of others. His new career may not earn him a lot more than his present job, but it will provide him with much more satisfaction and happiness.

Once you've determined that your team member is dissatisfied, you want to ask yourself, "How motivated is he or she to improve his or her circumstances?" Countless people aren't happy with their careers, but far fewer will do something about it. You want people on your team who have figured out that they're trapped in the boxed life and who will do whatever it takes to improve their circumstances. These individuals are likely to work hard and follow our system.

7. Ambition

I call this the "get it done" mentality. Team members enter our business to improve their lives. You want individuals who dream big and set goals for themselves. They'll commit whatever time and effort are required in order to accomplish their objectives. Rather than see obstacles as setbacks, they view them as opportunities to learn and grow. They realize that success is no accident—it requires hard work—and they're willing to "get things done, no matter what." When they face difficult times, they refuse to give up. They seek the support of others and do whatever it takes to find solutions to their problems.

You want individuals whose actions match what they say they'll do. If they commit to meeting a certain goal, they'll complete all the smaller tasks required to reach bigger objectives. As I've shared in other items on the 7 Point List, they have an ownership mentality. In this case, it means that they never give up and that they are self-motivated.

Leadership Is Within Your Reach

Too many of us have incorrect beliefs about leaders. It's easy to think that the famous leaders we've seen on TV and read about in books were born with amazing gifts that we could never have. This makes it seem as though leadership is something you're either born with or not, which can make it easy to make excuses such as, "I don't have natural leadership skills, so I'll never be a good leader." *But the truth is that most good leaders worked very hard to accomplish their goals,* which means that with an equal amount of effort, leadership is within your grasp as well.

We not only figured out what makes a good leader in our business, but we also made it simple to learn and duplicate. Our system turns ordinary people into leaders. And our approach relies on teamwork. An essential part of being a leader is the ability to work with those with the highest potential to become leaders and the ability to build a team. After using the 7 Point List to evaluate your team members, the next step is to figure out the best way to work with those team members. The **Leadership Layers** concept that you'll read about next will be your guide as you determine the roles that your team members will play on your team.

Chapter 21

Leadership Layers

The **Leadership Layers** concept is something that we use to help you to figure out how each member of your team can effectively help the rest of the team. Once you introduce new team members to your business, it's important to figure out where, among the following three categories, to place your new team members:

- **Layer 1: Your Right Hand**
- **Layer 2: The Middle Layer**
- **Layer 3: The Front Line**

Chain of Command

Every large organization has a chain of command that determines the roles and responsibilities of each team member. In the U.S. government, the chain of command has the president at the top. Beneath him is the vice president, followed by the Speaker of the House. This structure is also important to running an efficient large organization. This type of "chain of command" concept has stood the test of time, and it's useful because it splits up responsibilities and gives clear direction on who "steps up" in the event that one of the other leaders is not available.

Allow me to use a restaurant to give you another example of how leadership layers work in our business. In a fancy restaurant, there are normally many chefs who work together to create a great meal in a short amount of time. Just as one successful restaurant has several chefs who work together to achieve a common goal, we also have categories for our team members. In most big kitchens, the *executive chef* is responsible for running the entire kitchen. In our business, this would be the "leader" of a team. In addition to an executive chef, an advanced kitchen usually has the following roles:

1. **Sous-chefs** (sub-chefs) are trained to act in place of an executive chef. Our version of a sous-chef is called a "Right Hand."

2. **Station chefs** are below sous-chefs. They are responsible for a specific part of the cooking process and making sure everything runs smoothly for that section. We call this position the "Middle Layer."

3. **Basic chefs** are responsible for learning from the station chefs and helping the rest of the kitchen. We call team members in this position the "Front Line."

Beyond the Restaurant Comparison

The chain of command within a restaurant is a clear way to explain one of the most important roles of leadership layers. But it's an incomplete description because leadership layers aren't about who is the boss of whom.

For instance, if you have your own team, you are its leader. But you are also part of another team, and that team is part of the larger organization. *You may be the leader of one team and the Middle Layer in another, larger team.* Thus, throughout your career, you'll always play multiple roles—no matter how much you accomplish. So any feelings of "I'm higher up than you, which means I'm more important," don't fit how our business works.

In fact, an aspect of Trust and Understanding is that we believe we're all in this together, supporting each other and helping one another to succeed. Although some have more experience and lead large teams, each team member plays a key role in the entire organization's success, and in this way we're all equal.

Layer 1: Right Hand

The Right Hand on a team can be one person or multiple people if someone has more than one team. With the exception of the leader him- or herself, a leader's Right Hand has the highest potential for growth on a team. As a leader's abilities improve, a Right Hand's abilities improve as well. Leaders know their Right Hands well, they share common goals, and Right Hands aspire to be more like their leaders. As leaders progress in their careers, so do their Right Hands. Right Hands are driven, motivated, and know the details of their leader's businesses, and both share the same vision for their teams. If, for whatever reason, a leader isn't available to their team members, Right Hands can take their place and guide others.

Good Cop, Bad Cop and the Triangle of Trust

In the **good cop and bad cop** scenario, two people play different roles in order to reach a common goal. Imagine that someone has been arrested for stealing cigarettes at a convenience store. The "good cop" is the person who pretends to take the side of the criminal, "protecting" him from the bad cop. The role of the "bad cop" is to be as aggressive as possible in order to scare the crook. The criminal begins to trust the good cop more, and as a result, he decides to follow the good cop's recommendations.

In order to illustrate the roles of the good cop and bad cop in our business, let's assume that you're a leader, and you have a Right Hand. As an effective leader, you've recruited many team members. Some of these individuals will be part of your natural market. This means that they are family members, friends, and colleagues that you may have known for years.

Imagine that you've recruited a sibling. Your sister, Samantha, is on your team, and she's generally performing as well as you had expected. At the same time, Samantha has bad habits that are getting in the way of her success. This is something that needs to be addressed, and as a leader it's your responsibility to make sure it happens.

But because of the nature of your relationship with Samantha, she'll mainly view any suggestions you provide as coming from a sibling rather than from her team's leader. As you can see, it's hard to maintain authority when your relationship with a team member is based on ties through family, friendship, or a previous work setting. Meanwhile, the last thing you want to do is to have your professional life conflict with your personal one. In this example, your recommendation to your sister may be ineffective, and it can also actually damage your relationship with her.

Enter your Right Hand and the **leverage exchange** (for more about the leverage exchange, see Chapter 8). In this example, Samantha is part of your natural market, but she's not part of your Right Hand's natural market. Thus, your Right Hand can play the role of "bad cop." In this situation, you can ask your Right Hand to deliver the advice to Samantha. Your sister will be much more likely to listen to the advice because it is coming from someone with more credibility. As a result, you're leveraging your Right Hand's credibility to get the results you cannot achieve by yourself.

In this section, I focused on how the "good cop and bad cop" technique applies to a leader's relationship with his or her Right Hand. But keep in mind that the "good cop and bad cop" technique can work whenever a complication arises from working with your natural market. Thus you can apply it to not only the Right Hand layer, but the Middle Layer and Front Line as well, both of which you'll learn about next.

Layer 2: The Middle Layer

The Middle Layer's primary responsibility is to make sure that the communication between team members is smooth. Those who are part of the Middle Layer ensure that the team is running at its best. Their role is to be a coordinator. For example, new team members are responsible for going through Basic Training and attending multiple meetings. Do your team members understand all aspect of building Trust and Understanding? Do they know when and where to attend meetings? The Middle Layer makes sure that all team members are kept up-to-date and understand what their roles are.

Some additional responsibilities of the Middle Layer are as follows:

1. Making sure that new team members are introduced to their team members
2. Addressing questions about the Basic Training and building Trust and Understanding

3. Addressing any other concerns that team members may have
4. Keeping team members informed about events
5. Making sure that new team members have the materials and information they need
6. Resolving or figure out how to resolve conflicts between team members
7. Relaying to the Right Hand, the team leader, or both any concerns that new team members have

If you're a leader, you interact with your Middle Layer directly. They make sure that the rest of your team is fulfilling your instructions and following the system. They make sure that all team members understand their roles and responsibilities, and they are responsible for coordinating your team.

Layer 3: Front Line

We use the term "serious people" to describe those who make up your Front Line. This part of your team will have the most people. They are serious about their commitment to the system, and they are serious about reaching their goals. You measure their level of commitment by holding them accountable: Are they fulfilling their promises? Are they taking the day-to-day steps to accomplish bigger goals? Your Front Line communicates regularly with those in the Middle Layer in order to contribute to the team and learn as much as possible about the business.

Don't Limit Layers to Just "Your Team"

In our business, your team (no matter how big) is part of a bigger team. And that bigger team is ultimately one piece of the entire organization. Because we're all working together to reach a common goal, you need to realize that leadership doesn't just come from your direct team. You can have individuals from teams outside yours fulfill any of the roles on your team. For instance, you may be the Right Hand who acts as the "bad cop" for the leader of another team. Another example may be that the leader of another team can be a Middle Layer in your team who helps coordinate your new team members because that person is skilled at training new people. However it happens, realize that you shouldn't limit leadership to only people inside your direct team.

Accept support and give help to other teams because we're all part of the same organization. These overlapping leadership layers between different teams allow everyone to benefit from the talented people throughout our business. And sharing our skills and talents makes the entire organization stronger. In the next chapter, you'll learn two principles that make leadership layers a lasting part of your business. By following the **Natural Teamwork** approach, the leadership layers will produce harmony within your team.

Chapter 22

The Natural Teamwork Approach

As a leader, your job is to bring together individuals who come from a wide range of backgrounds and personalities in order to meet common goals. To do this well is an enormous challenge, but with a solid system in place, it's possible to not only meet this objective but to accomplish it in a way that inspires everyone to do his or her best. In this chapter, you'll learn our Natural Teamwork Approach. It's the final part of our leadership system, and you'll gain the most benefit from it when you've successfully followed the leadership principles that you read about previously.

What Is the Natural Teamwork Approach?

When you think of the word *natural*, what comes to mind? Perhaps you think of nature, such as the outdoors. Or maybe you think of someone with "natural talent," like a gifted swimmer or musician. When we say "natural approach," we're describing a system that comes about without much effort . . . or so it appears. In fact, the seemingly effortless aspect has to do with the fact that you've worked really hard to reach this point.

The use of *natural* to describe our system applies to most skills as well. Although the gifted swimmer or musician may seem as if he or she performs effortlessly, it usually results from countless hours of training and practice that led to the performance looking so easy. When you follow our teamwork approach, the collaboration and support you and your team provide each other will appear effortless. An outsider may observe your team and ask, "Wow! How do they get along so well?" Without knowing any better, he or she may think it happened without any effort on your part. But what such teamwork really shows is your strict commitment to the system and your ability to teach it to your team members.

The natural teamwork approach is based on two principles:

1. Alignment
2. Accountability

Alignment

Imagine that you and two friends are planning to take a boat trip. You come together because the adventure will be more fun with friends than traveling alone. You also appreciate that you can leverage your different strengths: One friend read maps well, the other knows how to repair boats, and you are highly skilled at piloting vessels.

For months, the three of you have looked forward to traveling together. Once you are on the boat, however, you suddenly discover that no one wants to go to the same place. Despite having the combined skills to safely get practically anywhere by boat, no one is willing to let go of his or her personal agenda in order to benefit the other two. With no agreed-upon destination, you're left disappointed and stuck. As you can imagine, a trip like this would be a complete failure.

In our business, alignment involves people with different backgrounds and skills coming together to meet common goals—or to use the boat comparison above, *you're traveling to the same place.* Everyone strives to accomplish the same objectives, and you and your team members agree on *how* to do this. Furthermore, alignment means that everyone is following the system. But the moment one team member says, "I want to do things my way, regardless of whether or not it follows the system," your team is out of alignment, your leadership is weakened, and your entire team's success is at risk.

Our Ego Gets in the Way of Alignment

A remarkable quality of our business is that success is available to anyone who's willing to follow our system. Whether you were born rich or poor, or have advanced educational degrees or no degrees at all, opportunity awaits anyone who works hard and believes in our approach. Thus your team members reflect a wide range of backgrounds. New team members may be young or old, full of professional know-how or just starting out. Regardless of what experiences team members bring to your team, they must be prepared to drop their ego if it's keeping them from following the system. In fact, when an entire team is able to put the individual egos of its members aside, the team has dramatically increased its ability to grow.

Our ego can be a problem at any layer of business, not just at the level of new team members. Right Hands, the Middle Layers, and the Front Line—any of us can fall into the trap of letting our ego get in the way of accomplishing our goals.

So how do you identify when there is no alignment? The Leadership Layers are a guide. When alignment fails, you'll see a breakdown between the responsibilities of your Leadership Layers. For example, if your Front Line is consistently struggling to turn prospects into team members, clients, or both, there is most likely a communication problem between the Front Line and Middle Layers, Middle Layers and the Right Hand, or both.

Negative talk is another way to tell if there is a breakdown in alignment. For example, if the Front Line begins complaining about the Right Hand or the Right Hand criticizes a leader, a team is in trouble. This means that team members are distrusting the system, don't have Trust and Understanding, or both.

When alignment is collapsing, the best way to solve the problem is for the team's leader to stop the entire team's operation right away. If you're the leader, you must then find out what the problems are. Once you've figured out where your biggest roadblocks are, you're prepared to find the particular individuals who are the source of your team's misalignment. You can then work with these people to determine what their struggles are and the type of guidance they need from you.

Accountability

Allow me to illustrate what accountability means in the context of leadership by providing an example. Imagine that Amanda decided to hire a personal trainer. For years she had a gym membership, but she couldn't maintain a regular exercise routine.

Amanda finally committed to working with a personal trainer because she wanted someone to teach her how to exercise properly, help her set fitness goals, and help her maintain discipline.

Throughout their relationship, she and her personal trainer regularly communicated with each other. At the beginning of each training session, Amanda and her trainer reviewed the goals they had set the week before. Her trainer asked her questions such as, "How did you do this week?" and "What were the areas in which you felt successful, and were there any areas in which you struggled?"

During her training sessions, Amanda had someone to motivate and inspire her. Her trainer guided her and also carefully observed her actions to make sure that Amanda was exercising correctly.

At the end of each session, Amanda and her trainer set goals for the coming week. They also discussed the tasks that Amanda would need to complete between now and their next appointment. The moment Amanda left the gym, she knew exactly what she needed to do. And she knew that the next time she met with her trainer, the two of them would start their appointment by reviewing her progress.

As a leader, one of your responsibilities is to be like Amanda's personal trainer. Not only do you have to make sure that your team members understand what you expect from them, but you're also holding them responsible for following through with all the steps that are necessary to meet their goals.

Also, accountability isn't just about discussing goals. That would be like a personal trainer and his client spending every training session discussing fitness goals, diet, and weight loss without ever exercising. You can imagine what a waste of time that would be.

Leadership means that you hold your team members responsible for fulfilling their obligations. One way you do this is through regular meetings. For instance, team conference calls provide the ideal setting to hold your team members accountable. During a conference call, a leader will start a conversation with one or more team members. A leader and his or her team will establish goals, including personal ones that each individual will be responsible for fulfilling by the time they meet again.

During the next conference call, everyone will share what he or she accomplished since the last conversation. All participants know the goals of everyone else, so team members hold one another responsible for accomplishing what they promised to do. In this setting, it would be very awkward for a team member to say, "I was really busy, so I didn't get much done this week" when asked about what he or she accomplished since the last meeting. You can imagine how difficult it would be to confess this.

Alignment + Accountability = Harmony

At the beginning of this chapter, we explored the meaning of the Natural Teamwork Approach. It's a way to run your business where everyone cares for one another and a team's interaction appears effortless. When alignment and accountability work together, relationships among team members are rooted in Trust and Understanding, and harmony is the natural outcome.

Harmony is the result of hard work and focus. It requires your team's determination to meet mutual goals and follow the system. As you build your team, you strive to attain harmony. Without it, your team will not grow, you'll feel constant stress, and success will slip right past you. But once you experience it, you'll wonder how you could work any other way.

Harmony can be summed up by the saying, "We're all in this together." Each team member knows that he or she plays an important role in the entire team's success. All team members also recognize that without teamwork, everyone suffers. Just as leadership layers describe a team's relationship to the entire organization, harmony represents the Trust and Understanding that exists between every individual—regardless of his or her title.

We're nearing the end of our journey together. In the final chapter, you'll read about Amy. Her example points to the power of our team-building system. Although she didn't believe in it at first, she eventually discovered that every part of it was designed with her success in mind.

Chapter 23

Trust the System

Amy started off in the leadership business after years in the financial services industry. She had qualities that many of her colleagues wish they had: extensive knowledge about financial products and services, countless hours of sales experience, a solid track record of accomplishments, and a burning desire to help others. Those who started with no financial services background wanted to be more like Amy. And she knew it.

I could tell right away that she didn't fully trust our system. She questioned the approach too much and offered her ideas on how she could improve it. In addition, she believed that if she could make the system better, she'd gain even greater prestige within the organization. But I knew there was nothing she had been through that I hadn't. I had failed many more times throughout my career than she had. I had also overcome many more obstacles than she had.

Amy wanted her colleagues and me to acknowledge her efforts and to recognize that she could bring new methods to the system. But experience had taught me that she was wrong. So for three months, she tried to get my attention, and for three months I completely ignored her. It's not my usual style, but I knew that I'd never be able to convince her that her attempts were a waste of time. She'd never believe me if I said that her ego was slowing her down and that if she ignored rather than welcomed it, her success was guaranteed. Amy had too much thinking getting in the way.

For 90 days, Amy worked hard and did everything she felt she was supposed to do. To her disappointment, she accomplished very little. She was now at a low point—if things didn't improve, she was ready to give up. Amy wanted help and asked if we could meet. During our meetings, she described her struggles and frustrations. I could tell she had finally reached a point where she was ready to put her ego aside. In other words, I saw something in her that wasn't there before: humility.

I knew from this place of humbleness that she was ready to completely give up her effort to improve the system, which meant that she was ready to give in to our approach. That day, we had a great conversation during which she listened to my advice, and she committed to trusting the system 100 percent. Within weeks, her career had completely turned around. I asked Amy to explain the reason behind the dramatic change.

"From day one, I was told, 'Just follow the system.' It seemed fine, but it also sounded like advice that was meant for beginners. Not someone like me, who was an industry veteran," she said.

"Once prospective team members hear how our business can change their lives, they can't wait to sign up," I said. "But it seems like the moment they join, they quickly forget one of the most important parts of my message."

"What's that?" she asked.

"Whenever you begin questioning the system, you need to put those thoughts aside and fully trust our approach," I said.

"I think the problem is that it sounds too easy. In my case, I couldn't believe that success was as simple as following the system. I wanted it to be complicated, to be really difficult to learn—that was the sign of something really important," she said.

"And where did making things complicated lead you?" I asked.

"To nearly giving up," she said. Amy understood my point. She finally recognized that whether she agreed with the system or not at any given moment was not important. In the end, agreeing and disagreeing were just thoughts that were subject to change: One day she may be convinced that everything she was learning was the best way. The next day, she could feel as though nothing seemed right.

Thus when doubts came up, all she needed to do was to recognize that *anyone who had succeeded in this business had only done so by fully committing to the system.* They, like Amy, certainly had good days and bad, but regardless of feeling doubt or certainty, they continued to follow the system. In the meantime, those who failed most often did so because they refused to cast aside their distrust.

"You can spend hours and hours attending classes, read every book you can get your hands on, and try to figure out ways to improve our system. But in the end, these efforts may create more problems for your business than solutions. At some point, you have to let go of your questioning and doubtful mind and jump right into this business without hesitation," I said.

"And once I did that, I experienced faster results than I though possible," Amy said. "If I'd only known better, I wouldn't have wasted my time trying to reinvent the wheel."

Put Your Faith in Trust and Understanding

We've spent countless hours developing our approach, and we've given you one basic task: Commit to the system 100 percent and then duplicate it. Thoughts such as "That's way too easy," and "There has to be more to it" are thoughts that can kill a career before it even gets started.

Imagine that you were a soldier. How silly would it be if you were on the front lines and the moment you were told to fight back, you decided to put in place your own strategy for attack? "I know I was trained to do things a certain way, but I think my plan is better!" you insist. Your actions would put your entire group at risk, and they would show that you didn't fully believe in your leader's ability to guide you. The same goes for our business. Leave your doubts behind and direct all your energy toward following the system. For us, it's "act first, think later."

From the first chapter in this book to the last, you've learned about an approach to team building that can be summed up by three words: Trust and Understanding. In our business, leaders are made, not born, and our team-building system presents an opportunity to accomplish more than you thought possible and improve the lives of countless people.

Big Dreams

I'm certain you'll continually refer back to the lessons in this book because they'll provide valuable information throughout your career. And while the time we've spent together in this book is limited by the words you've read, our voyage will continue through the relationships that you build with your business mentor, team members, clients, and everyone else you will meet during your career.

Throughout the life of your business, you'll experience many moments of joy as well as times when you'll believe that you've failed. Whenever you feel discouraged, remind yourself why you launched this career in the first place. Recognize that any setback you face in the present is only one experience that you will learn from as you work toward achieving your dreams. One of the most powerful aspects of our system of Trust and Understanding is that it's designed for long-term growth. Obstacles will come your way, but as you progress through your career, your achievements will be greater than any disappointments.

My greatest wish for you is that your career provides you many years of fulfillment. I hope it motivates you to overcome any self-limiting beliefs you have about yourself. Like anything worth having in life, success will require focus and hard work. Whenever you experience setbacks, continually remind yourself of others who have made their greatest hopes a reality by using the ideas and concepts I have written about here. There's no big secret to their success. It required following the principles of Trust and Understanding. Here's to a career full of big dreams and even bigger accomplishments.